S P I R I T U A L

A T H E I S M

S P I R I T U A L

A T H E I S M

S T E V E   A N T I N O F F

COUNTERPOINT
BERKELEY

Library of Congress Cataloging-in-Publication Data

Antinoff, Steve.
  Spiritual atheism / by Steve Antinoff.
      p. cm.
  ISBN-13: 978-1-58243-564-0
  ISBN-10: 1-58243-564-2
  1. Atheism. 2. Spirituality. 3. Religion. I. Title.

  BL2747.3.A69 2010
  211'.7—dc22

2009038161

Cover design by David Bullen
Interior design by Megan Jones Design

Printed in the United States of America

COUNTERPOINT
2117 Fourth Street
Suite D
Berkeley, CA 94710

www.counterpointpress.com

Distributed by Publishers Group West

10 9 8 7 6 5 4 3 2 1

PART 1

READING KAFKA FOR BREAKFAST, SWALLOWED UP FOR LUNCH

"GOD IS NECESSARY, AND SO MUST EXIST . . . YET I KNOW THAT HE DOESN'T EXIST, AND CAN'T EXIST."

—KIRILOV, IN DOSTOYEVSKY'S *THE DEVILS*

OVER THE LAST hundred and sixty years a great dilemma has been hatching out of western spiritual consciousness. Western woman and man have drawn an X through the world. Through ourselves and through our world.

Traces of this momentous act can be found in the apparently detached but finally desperate warning of Kierkegaard's "aesthete" in his book *Either/Or*: "Do it or don't do it—you will regret both." In Kierkegaard's: "I feel as if I were a piece in a game of chess, when my opponent says of it: 'That piece cannot be moved.'" In Kierkegaard's: "I have never at any moment of my life been deserted by the faith that one can do what one will—only one thing excepted, all else unconditionally, but one thing not, to throw off the melancholy in whose power I was."[1]

Traces can be found in Nietzsche's remark: "Behind every great human destiny there sounded as a refrain a yet greater 'in vain'" and in his contention that with the death of God we have "unchained this earth from its sun" and are "plunging continually"—"straying as through an infinite nothing."[2]

Traces can be found in Kafka's 1920 aphorism: "He has the feeling that merely by being alive he is blocking his own way." In Kafka's: "His own frontal bone blocks his way (he bloodies his brow by beating against his own brow)." In his: "A cage went in search of a bird," and in the man-ape's explication of that cage in his story "A Report to an Academy" that reads: The "cage . . . was too low to stand up in and too narrow to sit down."

Traces can be found in August Strindberg's lines from *A Madman's Defense*: "The bond that binds me is not a chain of iron that I could break off, it is a cable of rubber that stretches itself. The harder it is stretched, the more violently it pulls me back to my point of departure." In Paul Tillich's: "The situation of existence cannot be overcome in the power of this situation. Every attempt to do so strengthens this situation, which can be summed up in the title of Sartre's play, *No Exit*."

Traces can be found in the nurse's remark to Meursault in the opening pages of Camus's *The Stranger*: "If you go slowly you get sunstroke. But if you go fast, you work up a sweat and catch a chill," and in Meursault's comment: "She was right. There is no way out." And in Meursault's later realization: "To stay or to go, it amounted to the same thing."

Traces can be found in the closing lines of Beckett's *The Unnamable*: "I don't know, I'll never know, in the silence you don't know, you must go on, I can't go on, I'll go on." In the celebrated line that opens *Waiting for Godot*: "Nothing to be done." In Beckett's remark to his friend, art historian George Duthuit, that self-expression in our time is "the expression that there is nothing to express, nothing with which to express, nothing from which to express, no power to express, no desire to express, together with the obligation to express."

In the Zen tradition, paradoxes such as these are called koan. A koan is a challenge, in the form of a dilemma, given by a Zen master to a disciple. But the koan poses no ordinary challenge, for the dilemma to which it points is a special kind of dilemma, a dilemma which *must* be resolved if the recipient of the challenge is ever to find peace, liberation, or happiness, yet which he or she finds impossible to resolve. Typical examples of koan are:

- If you utter a word I will give you thirty blows; if you utter not a word, just the same, thirty blows on your head.

- When you meet a wise man on your way, if you do not speak to him or remain silent, how would you interview him?

STEVE ANTINOFF

- Assertion prevails not, nor does denial. When neither of them is to the point, what would you say?

- [The dying Shakyamuni Buddha is held to have said:] If anyone among you should say that I am now entering into nirvana, he will not be my disciple. Nor will he be my disciple who should say that I am not entering nirvana.

- Call this a *shippe* [a stick sometimes carried by Zen teachers, especially in the *sanzen* (interview) room] and you assert; call it not a *shippe* and you negate. Now, do not assert or negate and what would you call it? Speak, speak!

- A shackle if you sit, a shackle if you walk.

- If you wish to see the North Star, face south.

The obvious question, of course, is why anyone would waste his time struggling with a dilemma that seems impossible to solve. It truly would be a waste if the demand to resolve came solely from the arbitrary command of a Zen master. *So what* if I can't interview without speech or silence, can't see the North Star in the south? Why not give the old master the finger and walk off?

Because the master is secondary. Because the entire significance of the koan lies in the master's command being an externalized form of the disciple's own most fundamental inner demand—the demand for happiness, liberation, peace, and for an end to turbulence and vexation. For that reason alone are masters inessential. One can walk away from any master. One cannot walk away from one's own demand without paying the highest existential price.

This is what underlies the distinction Richard DeMartino,* one of the first western religious atheists, makes between what he calls the "natural koan" and the "given koan." The *natural koan* is the core question rising out of one's being, "out of the provocation of [one's] own life experience, already bestirred by some existentially oppressing perplexity." The *given koan* is supplied externally by the master when the "question" or "concern" that constitutes the natural koan has not yet been plumbed to its ultimate depth or when it lacks proper grounding or focus. But, DeMartino warns, "it must be emphasized that as long as the question or koan continues to be 'on the outside' or 'given,' the effort [to resolve it] is futile."[3] The binding power of

---

* DeMartino has been my teacher, and friend, for forty years; the most significant person in my adult life. I attended his lectures as a university student and for many years after. I am not a disciple. He had none. He once said (not referring to himself): "No genuine master wants a disciple. He wants you to be the master." A navy man during the Second World War, he was, as he once told me, "fighting a war of my own." He was part of the invasion force at the battle of Tinian Island, serving as a Japanese language interpreter. After the war he served as Historical Consultant to the Defense Panel of the International Military Tribunal for the Far East (the Tokyo War Crimes Tribunal). This enabled him to stay on in Japan where he studied with D. T. Suzuki, who encouraged him, given his temperament, to study with the more severe Zen man Shin'ichi Hisamatsu. In my observation, Zen Buddhism as something to gain an identity from or as an object to be attached to has meant nothing to DeMartino; Zen awakening, and its application to the real world, have meant everything.

the koan given from the outside by a "master" resides solely in its capacity to be superimposed on the koan burning naturally from within.

It is the argument of this book that the koan burning within the West, in western culture as a whole and in its individuals, has been given its most fundamental expression by Dostoyevsky, in the mouth of his great character Kirilov in the novel *The Devils*. "God," says Kirilov, "is necessary, and so must exist . . . Yet I know that he doesn't exist, and can't exist." These lines, first spoken in 1873, will plague us for the next thousand years. They form the koan that cannot be walked away from. Cannot be walked away from because they *are* the walker, even in his attempt to walk away. That is what Kirilov meant when he said: "Any other thinks, and then at once thinks something else. I cannot think something else. I think one thing all my life. God has tormented me all my life." That is why Kirilov, having proclaimed, in the hour before his suicide: "God is necessary, and so must exist . . . Yet I know that he doesn't exist, and can't exist," added, with his next breath: "But don't you understand that a man with two such ideas cannot go on living?"

2 THE UNTENABILITY OF GOD AND THE INSUFFICIENCY OF WOMAN/MAN

SPIRITUAL ATHEISM BEGINS with a triple realization: that our experience of ourselves and our world leaves us ultimately dissatisfied, that our dissatisfaction is intolerable and so must be broken through, and that there is no God. Kirilov is the herald of modernity's entrapment in that triple realization. "God is necessary, and so must exist," has meaning for him only because God "doesn't exist, and can't exist." The "must" refers back to Saint Augustine, who fifteen hundred years before Kirilov wrote famously in his *Confessions*: "Our heart is restless, until it repose in Thee."[4] For the spiritual atheist there is no Thee, making Augustine's words all the more true. The nonexistence of a Thee only strengthens the nonexistence of rest, or put conversely, only strengthens the existence of our restlessness. The nonexistence of God does not diminish human beings' spiritual need: mortal, finite human beings, unable to be satisfied in what is mortal and finite, long for the infinite. The most important question for the spiritual atheist, therefore, is whether it is possible to achieve the infinite, to transcend our finite, mortal condition, in a world without God.

Kirilov the atheist is at the opposite remove from the laughing men "who no longer believe in God" in Nietzsche's parable of the madman in his 1882 book *The Gay Science*. There, the bemused disbelievers—modern, rational, scientific—mock the madman's declaration that God is dead—"Has he emigrated? Has he gotten lost? Has he gone on vacation?" By contrast, Kirilov's atheism, though in accord with these men that God is, in Freud's words, an illusion, also presupposes Augustine's: "For I bore about a shattered and bleeding soul, impatient of being borne by me, yet where to repose it, I found not. Not in calm groves, not in games and music, nor in fragrant spots, nor in curious banquetings, nor in the pleasures of the bed and the couch; nor (finally) in books or poesy, found it repose."[5]

The inability to find repose within finitude is, of course, not exclusively the predicament of westerners. It has long been known, though today often enough obscured, in the East. The Taoist sage Chuang Tzu said centuries before Jesus' birth: "The 10,000 things ranged all around us and none of them is worthy to be our destination." The ancient Hindu texts the Upanishads assert: "There is no joy in the finite." In Buddhism, what is subject to old age, sickness, and death can never bring peace; in the words of the Zen master Shin'ichi Hisamatsu: "One can speak of long life, but as long as there is death, even if you live tens of thousands or millions of years, there will be no peace . . . True peace can only reside in truly being without life-and-death, in freeing oneself from life-and-death."[6]

Nonetheless, the death of God constitutes a pivotal moment for the West. For Nietzsche, God was the subconscious projection originating in the depths of the human need for spiritual self-preservation, the "antidote to practical and theoretical nihilism." The untenability of God forces the insufficiency of the finite, the insufficiency of the human, to center stage.

3 RELIGION REDEFINED

RICHARD DEMARTINO HAS said: "If you don't like the word *religion*, throw it out. But bear in mind there is a problem inherent in human existence that can't be resolved politically, economically, socially, historically, anthropologically, psychologically, artistically, or in any other way. The resolution of this problematic dimension that cannot be resolved by any of the ordinary resources of the human being I call religion. If you dislike that word, you can call it X."

4   RELIGIOUS ATHEISM IS NOT PSYCHOLOGY

THE INHERENT SUFFERING of human existence that is refractory to all attempts at resolution Tillich calls "existential anxiety." He distinguishes this from psychological (or "pathological") anxiety. "Pathological anxiety is a state of existential anxiety under special conditions."[7] Existential anxiety "belongs to existence," whether one is healthy or sick. Existential anxiety is not precipitated by any specific object, cause, or condition. It is unconditional; or, if you like, its precipitating condition is the human condition. For Tillich, therefore, its solution is not a therapy.

> Here we have the difference between the healing of an acute illness and the healing of the existential presuppositions of every disease and of every healthy existence. This is the basis for the healing of special acute illness, on this all groups agree. There are acute illnesses that

produce psychosomatic irregularities and destruction. There are compulsive restrictions of man's potentialities which lead to neurosis and eventually psychosis. But beyond this are the existential presuppositions. Neither Freudianism nor any purely existentialist consideration can heal these fundamental presuppositions. Many psychoanalysts try to do it. They try with their methods to overcome existential negativity, anxiety, estrangement, meaninglessness, or guilt. They deny that they are universal, that they are existential in this sense. They call all anxiety, all guilt, all emptiness, illnesses which can be overcome as any illness can be, and they try to remove them. But this is impossible. The existential structures cannot be healed by the most refined techniques. They are objects of salvation.[8]

Thus Kafka's aphorism: "Never again psychology!" When he writes: "He has the feeling that merely by being alive he is blocking his own way. From this obstruction, again, he derives the proof that he is alive," he is pointing not to some trauma in the psychosexual development of an individual, or to "conflicts between unconscious drives and repressive norms,"[9] but to the uncaused obstruction that I am to myself. To his Czech translator (and briefly his lover) Milena Jesenská, he writes:

You say, Milena, that you don't understand it. Try to understand it by calling it illness. It is one of the many manifestations of illness which psychoanalysis believes it uncovered. I do not call it illness and consider the therapeutic part of psychoanalysis a hopeless error. All these so-called illnesses, sad as they may appear, are facts of faith, efforts of people in distress to find moorings in maternal soil of some kind; hence psychoanalysis also considers the most fundamental origin of religions to be nothing but that which, in its opinion, causes the "illnesses" of the individual . . .

But moorings of the kind that take hold on solid ground are, after all, not some particular exchangeable property of man; rather, they preexist in man's nature and continue to form his nature (including his body) in this direction. And this they intend to cure?[10]

5 THE RELIGIOUS IMPULSE IN A WORLD WITHOUT GOD AND THE POSSIBILITY OF AN ATHEISTIC TRANSCENDENCE

THE ATHEIST WITH an ineradicable spiritual longing is the central concern of this book. The insufficiency of even the most profound, pleasurable, and meaningful human experiences drives us to search for a transformation, for an illumination of self that will resolve this insufficiency. The insufficiency is not psychological, a lack, say, of self-esteem, though it may have a psychological component. The solution of the psychological component may resolve many things. It does not resolve the insufficiency.

Richard DeMartino has written: "It is not that the ego has a problem. The ego is the problem." By ego he does not mean the Freudian ego but the English rendering of the Latin word for "I." The problem is nothing objective which besets the "I" but the "I" itself. That is why it is irresolvable in terms of the I. The attempt to do so Kafka describes in *He*: "His own frontal bone blocks his way (he bloodies his brow by beating against his own brow)." However formidable a barrier, in principle it can be smashed if sufficient force is brought against it. One may ram it with a helmet, or if that fails, a motorcycle, or if that fails, a truck. But what if the barrier is the one trying to ram through the barrier? Then one is blocked at the first move. The religious impulse arises out of the intersection of being blocked by the very one who cannot live without freeing oneself from being blocked. It "belongs to human existence" despite the nonexistence of God.

6 SPIRITUAL LONELINESS

Toward the end of the movie version of James Jones's novel *From Here to Eternity*, after Alma refuses Prewitt's proposal because she wants to marry someone "proper," she justifies her involvement with him, saying: "I do mean it when I say I need you. 'Cause I'm lonely. You think I'm lying, don't you?"

Prewitt responds: "Nobody ever lies about being lonely."

Loneliness, as the theologian Paul Tillich has said, "belongs to existence." It is as basic as the fear of death, to which it is related, for in every moment the inevitability of death reveals itself we know that we are ultimately alone. The pain of loneliness, when we allow it to strike us in its full power, is intolerable. For millions, who misapprehend its nature and its origin, it is a source of shame.

Loneliness begins in knowing "I" am "I." No one mistakes himself for someone else. In becoming "I," I open up an inner world that is uniquely mine and no one else's, an inner world that I alone "occupy." This is what William James means in saying that each of us breaks the universe at a unique point which we call "I."

No other person can do this for me. No one else can activate or experience my inner world from the inside. But not only do I experience myself as this center, I *must* do so. Knowing I am I is not simply a free act but a fact with which I am presented. I am I because of myself but also in spite of myself. I activate myself as I as an act of will, but I am also the recipient of myself against my will.

Nowhere is this more brutally brought home than in Edvard Munch's 1893 painting *The Scream*. The one doing the screaming (it has been argued whether it is male or female) has his hands over his ears. Yet the scream is not so much screamed as vomited. Vomited not so much from a spasm of the stomach but as a convulsion from the guts of the world. Munch confirms this in his diary: "One evening I was walking along a path, the city on one side and the fjord below. I felt tired and ill. I stopped and looked out over the fjord—the sun was setting and the clouds turning blood red. I sensed a scream passing through nature; it seemed to me that I heard the scream. I painted the picture; painted the clouds as actual blood. The color shrieked."

A shriek the screamer tries to block out. The hands hurrying toward the ears accomplish an astounding feat for a painting, moving its focal point from the shrieking energized colors to the colorless, invisible consciousness within the man. Human consciousness is the reality (or theme) of the painting, human consciousness in its basically paradoxical form.

In locating the origin of the scream in nature, Munch doesn't mean the cause of the scream is outside. The two other figures on the bridge hear nothing. Rather Munch indicates the scream originates deeper than the man's own personal psychology. It has a cosmic dimension that forces itself into consciousness against the man's will. Nonetheless the scream explodes through nature only through the consciousness of the man. He brings it into being. It could not exist without him. In hurrying to block out the scream, he is trying to block out his consciousness.

That's the paradox. His consciousness is what makes him who he is and no one else; it is his identity, and yet he has not chosen his consciousness but is its passive recipient. Though he is nothing without it, his consciousness, his screaming mind, is him despite himself.

The menace of the painting is that the screamer must bear the burdensome weight of this weightless consciousness. It is something he must contend with, *the fundamental thing* he must contend with, until he dies. Since no one else can occupy this inner point he calls "I" he must contend with it alone. My inner world, once activated, must ultimately be borne by me. The protagonists in Munch's world secretly know that it is not, finally, the absence of another that is loneliness, but the presence of oneself.

That is why self-identity and loneliness go together, why loneliness belongs to self-existence. No one can get outside of being inside. To be lonely is not a failure or a cause for shame but a fundamental aspect of human destiny. That does not make loneliness any easier to endure. Even in the "perfect" society one will still have to contend with one's mind. No one can escape the task of having to bear his or her inner world. The spouse, the parent, the lover, the friend can soften loneliness, temporarily diminish its edge, but as illness teaches, if all else fails, no one, finally, can step in as an understudy.

No one can get outside of being inside, yet as human beings we cannot be sustained or satisfied within ourselves. This was a point made by Richard DeMartino: as I, I am limited by, locked within, yet unfulfilled within myself. Hence the title of Carson McCullers's novel *The Heart Is a Lonely Hunter.* In the stunning film version, even more than the book, the saintly deaf-mute Mr. Singer is trapped within the unbearable silence of his own self-consciousness. His deafness reveals the human mind in nakedness; it presses him back into himself, deprives him of the protective buffers through which we humans ordinarily deny the degree of our disquiet. Neither his selflessness nor his astonishing compassion can protect him. None of the characters in the story can avoid the "hunt," or avoid loneliness despite their hunt. In *Who Is Man?* theologian Abraham Heschel writes: "The self is in need of a meaning which it cannot furnish itself." This drives it to seek in society what it cannot find within itself. Yet, Heschel adds, "Human existence cannot derive its ultimate meaning from society, because society itself is in need of a meaning."

One form of the spiritual quest is of course the hunt for that which puts an end to loneliness. In the words of Paul Tillich: "Our language has widely sensed the two sides of being alone. It has created the word 'loneliness' to express the pain of being alone. And it has created the word 'solitude' to express the glory of being alone." Jiddu Krishnamurti in his essay "The Need to Be Alone"[11] describes the evasion of loneliness as the motivating behavior of human beings and the depth mood beneath the symptomatic moods of boredom, and insists the real treasure of human existence lies in an Aloneness without loneliness, realized by confronting loneliness and going beyond it. Plotinus famously described his ecstatic mystical experience as the "flight of the alone to the Alone." The Zen master Pai-chang, asked what is the most extraordinary affair, replied: "Sitting alone on Ta-Hsiung Peak." How to shift the default mode of human existence from pain to glory, from loneliness to Aloneness, is the heartrending question. Nietzsche said he was the first lonely man. He did not mean he was the first to know loneliness but the first to be without God: from now on the battle with ultimate loneliness would have to be fought alone.

THE FAILURE OF SEXUAL LOVE TO SATISFY THE ULTIMATE SPIRITUAL LONGING

No ONE CAN get outside of being inside, yet as human beings we cannot be sustained or fulfilled within ourselves. In this dilemma originates the peculiarly human dimension of sexual love. A dimension which itself is a dilemma. Loneliness drives us into the arms of the other with a force at least equal to the drive for procreation. For human sexuality is never simply the drive to procreate. It is also the drive to create selves rid of their isolation. Since isolation is inherent in being an "I," the drive to be rid of isolation is also the drive to be rid of self, but to be rid of self, paradoxically, so as to gain oneself. Richard DeMartino, quoting Jesus' statement that one must lose oneself to find oneself, argued in his class lectures that this losing/finding was the key to understanding human sexual life. The longing to lose oneself so as to find oneself is the common root of the religious and sexual impulse in human existence. DeMartino often remarked on the religious origin of the word *ecstasy*, and in class when he would break out in song with Sinatra's "Let's get lost, lost in each other's arms," it was always in the context of the death–rebirth motif common to so many mystical and religious descriptions.

Consider the seventeenth-century Japanese Zen master Hakuin on the Zen breakthrough:

> It is the same with the student of Zen . . . All of a sudden he finds his body and mind wiped out of existence, together with the koan. This is what is known as "letting go your hold." As you become awakened from the stupor and regain your breath it is like drinking water and knowing for yourself that it is cold. It will be a joy inexpressible.[12]

There is a parallel dynamic in D. H. Lawrence's exploration of sexual love. In *Lady Chatterley's Lover* Connie's annihilation and rebirth are described: "she knew herself touched, the consummation was upon her, and she was gone. She was gone, she was not, and she was born: a woman."[13] And in *Women in Love:* "But, [Ursula] said gravely, 'didn't you say you wanted something that was *not* love—something beyond love?' 'I don't want love,' [Birkin] said. 'I don't want to know you. I want to be gone out of myself, and you to be lost to yourself, so we are found different.'"[14]

The obvious question, and many of us ask it repeatedly and existentially throughout our lives, is whether the fulfillment of the longing for romantic ecstasy in either of its fundamental forms (to be driven beyond oneself, or to be penetrated such that one's lonely center, which can be entered by no other, is, through the mystery of love, entered nonetheless) *truly* heals.

Consider the following figures, each of whom confronts the question of ecstasy, if not salvation, through love.

MARCEL PROUST

"We live only with what we do not love, with what we have brought to live with us only in order to kill the intolerable love." These troubling lines from volume five of *In Search of Lost Time* occur after the narrator has brought the elusive Albertine to live at his home. The words reflect a dilemma exposed by U.S. divorce rates, and its essence is this: Anxiety and uncertainty are prerequisites of the passion we call love. The roller coaster of anxious passion being tough to endure, we exert ourselves to make the beloved "ours" in order to again be calm, but in eliminating the anxiety we destroy the love. There is, as Proust says, "no peace of mind in love." It is an "incurable malady," accompanied by a "permanent strain of suffering."

And since "love is kept in existence only by painful anxiety," it is not necessarily the physically beautiful that keep one enthralled but those he calls "the fugitives." These are the lovers characterized by the eternal elusiveness that Proust calls "speed." They are aloof, unreliable, at least a touch mendacious, impossible to control. Such qualities imbue the fugitives with "the permanent possibility of danger," without which love soon degenerates into habit.

Yet while these "fugitive" lovers ignite the passions, the crux of Proust's understanding of love relations is that they, too, are not the true object of our desire, but only its catalyst. For Proust it is an illusion that love exists outside ourselves. The beloved whom we deem necessary to our lives is "simply an accident placed in the path of our surging desires," desires made up of the need to escape the anxiety, the insecurity, the lonely interiority that come with being a conscious self. The fugitives are those who heighten these desires in us most intensely, and yet our feeling and actions, he suggests, "bear no close and necessary relation" to those we love, but splash to one side of them "like the incoming tide breaking against the rocks."

Only when "we perceive that our love is a function of our sorrow, that our love perhaps is our sorrow, and that its object is only to a very small extent the girl with the raven hair," do we understand what gives rise to what Proust calls "the terrible need of another person."

RAINER MARIA RILKE

The ambiguity of the kiss, of the "shattering contact" of sexual love and its relationship to ultimate reality, is one of Rilke's great concerns, above all in his *Duino Elegies*. The completion of the *Elegies* became the central task of his life; the ten poems took him ten years (1912–1922) to write. The quest for an ecstatic penetration of infinity, which would heal women and men from the conflict concomitant with finitude, lies at its heart. Great love gives a glimpse of infinity, thus we seek it in love, but the lovers block each other's path. "Lovers, if the beloved were not there blocking the view, are close to it, and marvel . . . As if by some mistake, it opens up for them behind each other . . . But neither can move past the other, and it changes back to World," which for Rilke is the world of finite objects against which we are perennially opposed. "Forever turned toward objects, we see in them the mere reflection of the realm of freedom, which we have dimmed . . . That is what fate means: to be opposite, to be opposite and nothing else, forever." (*The Eighth Elegy*) It is this fate of lifelong opposition to the world and to ourselves that lovers futilely seek to evade. "Alas, with each other they only conceal their lot." (*The First Elegy*) "[Y]ou so blissfully touch . . . Until your embraces almost promise eternity. Yet, when you've once withstood the startled first encounter . . . and that first walk, just once, through the garden together: Lovers, are you the same? When you lift yourselves to each other's lips—drink unto drink—oh, how strangely the drinker eludes his part." (*The Second Elegy*) One of Rilke's English translators, J. B. Leishman, says in his commentary on the poems that for Rilke "[Love's] passion and hunger cannot and should not . . . be satisfied by the object that awakens it; it is for something infinite . . . it can find its fulfillment only in 'the Whole.'"[15] Disappointment in the finite beloved is intrinsic. The "shattering contact" of the kiss (*The Third Elegy*) beckons the lover beyond the beloved; the terrors unleashed through the difficulty of achieving what is glimpsed prompt the lover to escape once more back into the beloved, but at the cost of a squandered life. "Of course, he *wants* to escape, and he does; relieved, he nestles into your sheltering heart, takes hold, and begins himself. But did he ever begin himself, really?" (*The Third Elegy*)[16]

EDVARD MUNCH

In Munch's *The Scream* (1893), the fact that the other two people on the bridge hear nothing means it is possible to interpret the turmoil in the screamer's consciousness psychologically rather than existentially; as an anxiety peculiar to the screamer to which the others are immune. Two related paintings show this is not Munch's intent. In *Anxiety* (1894), several people are walking across the same bridge stretched over the same abysmal waters as in *The Scream*. The ominous blood-red landscape is virtually the same. In *Anxiety*, however, immunity does not exist. The disquiet is universal. All are plagued. In *Spring Evening on Karl Johan Street* (1891–92) the turmoil, the isolation, have infested the whole of the city. The viewer sees a procession of humanity out for an evening's pleasure yet undermined by the mind's anguish. No one relates to anybody; no sense of community exists except as a community of lonely damned. All face front, with no cognizance of their neighbor's existence and agony, as if hastening toward their own mass execution. In his diary Munch wrote: "I saw through them, and there was suffering in them all. Pale corpses who without rest ran along a twisted road at the end of which was a grave." It is inevitable, and borne out by many of his other works of the period, that their loneliness and dread drive them toward one another. In some of the most devastating love paintings ever made Munch's men and women seek refuge in each other from their own inner world, but since the consciousness of the beloved bears the identical burden and is driven by the identical need, his lovers are doomed to isolation. Always in these works the lover is pressed back into the lonely interiority he and she sought to evade. In *Ashes* (1894), the structural failure between human consciousness and coitus is driven in like a nail. The eyes of the man and the woman, dressed again after sex in the forest, no longer see one another but are locked onto the disappointment of their resurgent dread. Munch's biographer, J. P. Hodin, writes of it:

> We see . . . in *Ashes* (1894) the despair and emptiness after fleshly union, as though nature had betrayed men by promising them bliss and fulfillment, while in truth the biological force that urges them together is satisfied, and as individuals they are left empty. It is as if Schopenhauer's *Metaphysics of Sexual Love* were represented in the medium of painting. Man and woman are like elements which come into contact, obsess one another but cannot become united.

Of Munch's *The Lonely Ones (Two People)* (1895), Hodin writes:

> In the end there is loneliness. *The Lonely Ones (Two People)* are depicted standing silently on the beach. What they had sought was too beautiful, too pure, and too perfect. They longed for unity of soul, for deliverance from loneliness. They stand on the shore, the sea sings its eternal melody as an accompaniment to their pain-filled thoughts.[17]

Even when the seascape is serene, as in *Evening (Melancholy)* (1896), consciousness is beached within the enforced deliberation of itself. His couples copulate, never for reproduction, not

even for pleasure, but as the struggle of two inner contempla-
tions. They kiss in exquisite Nordic forests, or stand together by
the sea, bearing out the words of Munch's fellow Scandinavian,
Kierkegaard: "I feel as if I were a piece in a game of chess, when
my opponent says of it: 'That piece cannot be moved.'"

OSKAR KOKOSCHKA'S *THE TEMPEST* (*BRIDE OF THE WIND*) (1913)

A man lies with a woman in this painting, not on a bed but
in a boat splitting apart in whirling space. They have finished
intercourse. She sleeps against his shoulder, turned toward him,
transported by her love. He is on his back; not one centimeter of
him is inclined to her. Her flesh is soft. His is tense and knotted.
Her eyes close in sleep; *his* are like kicked-open doors. It is the
greatest painting of ambivalence about sex and love ever produced. The greatest portrayal in paint of the betrayal of love—
not betrayal by a lover but by love—ever produced. Ecstasy and
consummation have driven the woman (Alma Mahler, widow
of the composer Gustav Mahler) to sleep. They have driven the
man to insomnia, alertness, alarm. The ecstasy that has driven
him beyond himself has driven him beyond the both of them as
well. He is alone, eyes pulled open in the horrendous consciousness that in the midst of their embrace he has slipped out of
their embrace against his will. The illusion of sex is broken. The

embrace was the sole hope for what Charles Olson called "relief from the constant hammering." The embrace lied.

No cuckold has ever been betrayed as he is betrayed by his opened eyes. And tomorrow he will pull her to him again. "Past reason hunted, and no sooner had / Past reason hated," writes Shakespeare in Sonnet 129. Spiritual atheism begins with the realization that we cannot be fulfilled through another, and cannot be fulfilled through ourselves. "Marry or do not marry," says Kierkegaard, "you'll regret both."

8 THE FAILURE OF ARTISTIC CREATIVITY TO SATISFY THE ULTIMATE SPIRITUAL LONGING

THERE IS AN awful thought lying in ambush for the reader of Michelangelo's 1552 poem, written at age seventy-seven:

In such slavery,
and with so much boredom,
and with false conceptions and great peril
to my soul,
to be here sculpting divine things.

The "divine things" he sculpts are not divine simply because his chosen subject matter is Moses or a pietà. They are divine by virtue of his talent, and he knew it. He is chiseling away at the most sublime level of creativity and yet his soul is in grievous peril. How can that be? This small verse expresses the terror, the grief of the tragic relationship between subject and object, between the artist creator and the object the artist creates. No work of art is simply object; it is invested with the subjectivity of its creator. Yet the agony of Michelangelo's poem derives from his realization that between himself and all he creates there is an inherent gap. Even the subjectivity or "self" invested in the art object becomes an object to the subjectivity of the artist. He is not, finally, "in" what he creates but is, in effect, left behind. Just as the lover slips out from his own embrace, the artist slips out of his own creative act. No artist can be saved by his creation, however highly esteemed by himself or by humankind. That is why it is possible to experience emptiness in the midst or aftermath of great applause.

Aldous Huxley's remark, "There comes a time when one asks even of Shakespeare, even of Beethoven, is that all?" is a threat not only to the appreciators of masterpieces, who search for an ultimate meaning through the highest achievements and insights of human culture, but, far more significantly, is a threat to the creators of these achievements. Gustav Mahler, who according to his friend, the conductor Bruno Walter, was obsessed by the urgent need to find salvation his entire life, confessed at the time of the composition of his Symphony No. 8 that his music could not save him. Picasso after a lifetime of masterpieces threw himself into a frenzy of creation in a futile attempt to hold old age and death at bay. In his eighties, Toscanini wrote: "I am so tired of being called Maestro Arturo Toscanini that it bores me to even read my own name." Martha Graham, who asserted, "eternal vision is the only antidote to the oblivion that is death," fell into alcoholism and depression when age and arthritis finally drove home, despite the denial which turned her performances into embarrassment, that she could not dance eternally. The day her handpicked successor replaced her in *Appalachian Spring* Graham told her: "You must know that this is the worst day of my life."

Her observation that the "eternal vision is the only antidote to the oblivion that is death" lies at the root of conflict inherent in the spiritual quest through art. The masterpiece—the work, that is, whose value is eternal—embraces the hope of the artist to find something greater than transiency, finitude, and death. That hope is realistic if what is sought is an affirmation of life or self greater than the forces that threaten to negate it *while still remaining in the grip of these forces*. The hope is illusory if what is sought is liberation. The hope that the predicament of the subject-artist, left stranded, finally, by his or her object-creation, will be overcome by the affirmation of the work's appreciators is likewise illusory: a standing ovation by the whole of humanity for the duration of time would, for all its value, leave the creator unfulfilled. Kierkegaard's "whether thy name be remembered as long as the world stands (and so was remembered as long as the world stood)"[18] expresses the impossibility of finite beings solving the problem of finitude by finite means. This is why the seventy-nine-year-old Michelangelo, in a shocking sonnet written in 1554, called art idolatry. Eugène Delacroix cited the poem in his own journal on January 4, 1824:

> Here is what the great Michelangelo wrote on the brink of the grave: "Borne on a frail bark in the middle of a stormy sea, I draw near the close of my life. I touch the common bourne where everyone goes to account for the good or evil that he has done. Ah! how clearly I now perceive that art, my idol, the tyrant of my imagination, plunged it in error . . . No, sculpture, painting, cannot suffice to calm a soul turned toward divine love, a soul laved by sacred fire."[19]

A lifetime of masterpieces—whose greatness will be affirmed as long as humans populate the earth—could not calm his soul.

THE CASE OF MARK TWAIN

In the weeks before the seventy-one-year-old Samuel Clemens sailed for Oxford to receive an honorary degree, he was troubled by a dream. Attending an important gathering, he finds he is wearing only his nightclothes, and though he tries to explain, "I am Mark Twain!" no one takes any notice.

Why was it necessary for arguably the most famous man in the world, author of masterpieces and adored by nations and kings, to still shout out his identity, and to be tortured by the anxiety of not being recognized? How much greatness, whether in quantity or quality, must be achieved for even the genius to reach a definitive affirmation of self that cannot be diminished or destroyed by the rejection or indifference of others?

Clemens's first biographer, Albert Bigelow Paine, relates that when the two men descended in a hotel elevator that opened directly into the dining room, the disappointed author insisted they go back upstairs and take another elevator that enabled him to make a grand entrance down the stairs into the crowded lobby before reaching their table. Another biographer asserts Clemens spent the last ten years of his life in an endless search for adulation. Yet would a psychologist's analysis of this pathological insecurity fully explain Clemens's disturbing dream?

At the peak of his popularity Clemens confided to a notebook: "My books are water; those of the great geniuses are wine. Everybody drinks water." Why is the turning of the wine they have made back into water the tragic anti-miracle of so many creative minds? The concluding page of his most serious late fiction, *The Mysterious Stranger*, suggests Twain understood this tragedy not as the offshoot of some psychological disturbance but as an intrinsic relationship between the mind and what it produces. "Nothing exists," the protagonist is told, and knows it to be true, "all is a dream, God—man—the world—the sun . . . *Nothing exists save empty space—and you*. And you are

41

not you—you have no body, no blood, no bones—you are but a *thought* . . . alone in shoreless space . . . without friend or comrade forever . . . It is all a dream—a grotesque and foolish dream. Nothing exists but you. And you are but a *thought*—a vagrant thought, a useless thought, a homeless thought, wandering forlorn among the empty eternities."[20]

For Twain these words were far from fiction. They echo almost verbatim a letter he wrote after the death of his wife in which he confesses they describe his daily experience. It is natural, then, that he found that his creations—his books and all he poured into them; his alter ego Mark Twain and all he poured into *him*—were created, and then in some sense swallowed up in an empty well, wine reduced to water, forcing him to scream in his dream—inaudibly: "I am Mark Twain!"

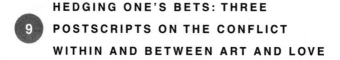

HEDGING ONE'S BETS: THREE POSTSCRIPTS ON THE CONFLICT WITHIN AND BETWEEN ART AND LOVE

OSKAR KOKOSCHKA REVISITED

In Kokoschka's *The Tempest* (also known as *Bride of the Wind*), Alma Mahler sleeps on the shoulder not simply of a man but of an artist: Kokoschka himself. We know from the discussions he had with his biographer J. P. Hodin that he felt his passion for her could destroy him as a painter: "In his painting *The Tempest* (1914), he depicted himself experiencing the torment in the struggle between his calling as an artist and love, creativeness and sex."[21] Look at his face and body: this is a painting of a creator whose art gives him no rest, whose untenability as a man, despite his art, drives him to love. Love gives him no rest but threatens his art. In the world of this painting, neither art nor love—nor their abandonment—will do.

STEVE ANTINOFF

STEPHEN SONDHEIM'S *SUNDAY IN THE PARK WITH GEORGE*

The Georges Seurat of the musical *Sunday in the Park with George* will always choose art over love. He has no illusions that love will remove loneliness but love can soften its edge. Rather than forgo that softening he will without scruple condemn the woman he loves to the very loneliness that he seeks to ease in himself, *so long as she stays with him of her own volition.* In that one sense he is a moralist, refusing to influence his lover to abandon her plan to leave him and move to America. Otherwise, that she is, as she sings, "diminished with him and without him," counts for little against the loneliness which urged him to draw her, and her successor, toward him. His is the weakness of all those willing to make someone love them for the primary purpose of being strong alone.

THE CASE OF GUSTAVE FLAUBERT

"For me, love is not and should not be in the foreground of life; it has to stay in the back of the shop." This Flaubert wrote to his married mistress, Louise Colet, when she pressed for greater commitment. "Love for me is not the first thing in life, but the second. It is a bed where one puts one's heart to take a rest. But one doesn't stay lying down all day."

The *first thing in life,* of course, was to write, which he regarded as a monkish vocation requiring the sacrifice of all else. And so he lived his life as a recluse in his provincial home, Croisset, where, as one of his biographers put it, "He shut himself up . . . with the illustrious dead for company, to devote himself to the worship of art."

Flaubert saw bachelorhood as essential to creativity. Art permitted no divided allegiances. He wrote: "For me, the true poet is a priest. As soon as he takes holy orders and puts on his cassock, he must leave his family." Nonetheless, the religious quality of his artistic quest was ambiguous. "I love my work with a frenzied and perverted passion as the ascetic loves the hair shirt which scratches his belly."

When alone and sick he regretted to his close friend George Sand that he lacked the house filled with children that she enjoyed. He leased rooms in Paris, to be with his niece and her husband, "for," as he wrote Sand, "I cannot stand being alone anymore." His niece records in her memoir that after she and her uncle made a Sunday visit to a woman and her children in the country, Flaubert confided that the woman, and by implication not he, was "in the right."

Yet Flaubert barely stayed in the rooms in Paris, returning almost at once to Croisset. He could not have lived as the woman "in the right" lived. As he once wrote: "Literature bores me utterly. But it's not my fault. With me it's become a sort of constitutional pox, and there's no getting rid of it. I'm stupefied with art and aesthetics, yet I can't live one day without scratching at the wound that's eating me away."[22]

THE FAILURE OF HUMAN
(10) EXPERIENCE TO SATISFY THE
ULTIMATE SPIRITUAL LONGING

THE GREAT WALL OF CHINA ENTERS A TEACUP

In my novel *The Atheists' Monastery* there is this conversation between the protagonist, Julius Cain, and the master of an unspecified religious order:

CAIN: "I ask you again: How have you achieved infinite liberation without God?"

MASTER: "In our monastery it is not God that satisfies the religious impulse of man."

CAIN: "I am here to know how it *is* satisfied."

MASTER: "To know this it is first best to know how it is dissatisfied. The ancient Master Chuang Tzu has said: 'The ten thousand things ranged all around us and not one is worthy to be our destination.' But ten thousand things are too many; this monastery sets before you one thing, *any* one thing—for example, drinking tea. Now there are schools, say, of Buddhism, which teach: when drinking tea be aware of drinking tea. Our Order teaches: To be aware of drinking tea is to be aware that you cannot drink the tea, of your inability to drink the tea, of the insufficiency of drinking tea. The act of drinking tea holds within it a great wall. The spiritual impulse is satisfied only by passing through the wall in the tea. For if a man could pass through one thing he could pass through all things. But he cannot pass through one thing. Not one. So he stops drinking the tea, you may suppose, moving on to something else. But the inability to drink the tea, its insufficiency, is at once the insufficiency of not drinking the tea. Realizing this, one knows the insufficiency of all acts, all things, all moments, all situations. In the act of meeting a man there is the wall of meeting a man. In the act of drying the hands: the wall of drying the hands. The act of beginning a conversation, of ending it, of never beginning it: all has within it the same great wall.

The great wall is the great wall of China. Not the wall that stretches from the Yellow Sea to the Gobi Desert. The wall that was "built" by those T'ang dynasty Chinese who first threw koan at the feet of humanity as Moses once threw the tablets of the Law. Those koan also have their law, though it is neither moral nor legal. Two laws, in fact. First: the law of the insufficiency of all things, including love, including art. Second: the splendor of all things, including love, including art. The second law holds true for those who have destroyed the first. The first is binding for those who have not destroyed it. For these the insufficiency of art, like the insufficiency of love, points back to the insufficiency of all human experience. I signaled out the lover and artist precisely because theirs are among the paths where what does not fall short is sought when it is realized that all "ordinary" experience falls short.

The assertion of the insufficiency, of the falling short, of all things, is bound to raise hackles and so needs to be explained. Things fall short only insofar as one seeks in them peace, happiness, liberation, ultimate meaning, and an end to loneliness and dissatisfaction. Nietzsche's "Behind every great human destiny there sounded as a refrain a yet greater 'in vain'" does not diminish the greatness of the "destiny" of a Shakespeare; it only asserts that his greatness could not overcome the ultimate meaninglessness of greatness *for the one who achieved it.* Kierkegaard surely understood this when he wrote that no man of his generation could get the upper hand on him and that he could achieve everything but the removal of his melancholy. The point is so powerfully formulated by Richard DeMartino in "The Human Situation and Zen Buddhism" that I quote at length here:

No role, function, or vocation can ever satisfy the human—male or female—as human. The ego, however, constrained by its inner contradiction to seek its completion, is beguiled by that contradiction into just that deception . . .

However truly great the husband, wife, parent, ruler, scientist, thinker, artist, professional or business man—or woman, however much richer such an ego is, however much more it has itself, it does not have itself fully as ego, nor has it realized itself ultimately as human.

Expressing genuine subjectivity in going out of itself and giving itself in love, creativity, devotion to an ideal, or dedication to a task, it continues to be bound to and dependent upon the particular object element of that expression—the specific loved one, artistic activity, ideal profession, or work . . . [I]ncapable of being a subject without an object, it is immediately curtailed and circumscribed by that object. Hence the ambivalence—in *eros* or *philia*—of the hidden or open hostility to that which is loved . . .

The ego, requiring an object to be a subject, can never attain complete fulfillment in or through any object. Such fulfillment, while authentic, is still limited, temporary, and tarnished. Despite the true richness of its creative subjectivity, the actual abundance of the contents of its life, the real greatness of its accomplishments and successes, the ego as ego is left unfulfilled. Unable to sustain itself within itself, and perhaps tormented by feelings of its own undeservedness, guilt, or sin, it comes to know melancholy and despondent moments of loneliness, frustration, or despair. Inwardly plagued by restlessness, insecurity, or a contempt and even hatred of itself, outwardly it possibly manifests any number of psychological or psychosomatic disturbances.[23]

I opened this book by calling the X that we have drawn through ourselves, despite ourselves, the great spiritual event of the last one hundred and sixty years. In that act the koan, born in the East, has come west. Kafka realized this and wrote the aphorism "He has the feeling that merely by being alive he is blocking his own way. From this obstruction, again, he derives the proof that he is alive." In it, as with all the "western koan" with which I began this book, the great wall in the teacup, always latent in the West, has sprung up in our midst. The insufficiency of self and world is disclosed in the insufficiency of any one act, any one thing. This is the meaning of Kafka's miniature story "The Knock at the Manor Gate." There, a man is condemned for knocking at a manor gate. Yet it is not he who knocked but his sister. Yet his sister did not knock but only brought her fist near the door. The problem of being a self, "the great matter of life and death," as Zen practitioners call it, blazes through the most minimal act, precedes the act, in fact, because the problem is one of being as well as one of doing.

In another miniature, "The Top," Kafka writes of a philosopher who disregards everything in the universe but a spinning top, having understood it was "uneconomical" to occupy himself with the many great problems with which philosophers usually contend, since "the understanding of any detail, that of a spinning-top, for instance, was sufficient for the understanding of all things." He thus lies in ambush wherever children are at play and when he spots a boy spinning a top goes in pursuit and tries to catch it. The koan resides in the inability to catch a spinning top without stopping it from spinning. What he finds in his hand with each attempt is "a silly piece of wood," which he throws to the ground, and walks away. His belief that in passing through the wall in one thing he would pass through the wall in all things is the philosopher's hope and obsession; that in failing to penetrate the top he is barred from everything in the universe is the philosopher's actuality and despair. But if everything in the universe is a blocked door, it is also an open one. Kafka himself writes in an aphorism: "There are countless hiding places, there is only one deliverance, but possibilities of deliverance are again as many as the hiding places." He echoes the twelfth-century Chinese Zen master Wu-men Hui-k'ai's saying that the Great Way has no gate; thus it can be entered from

everywhere. The title of Wu-men's book is *The Gateless Barrier.*
In the opening page he says that to attain the "wondrous awakening" the barrier without a gate must be passed through. The
barrier is not an object. The barrier is he or she who seeks to
pass through the barrier—the "I." Kafka understood this when
he wrote: "His own frontal bone blocks his way (he bloodies
his brow by beating against his own brow)." Any object-barrier
can be penetrated if one can bring enough force to bear, but if
the barrier is the subject or self bringing the force, what does
one do? Richard DeMartino writes: "The ego, in an existential
quandary which it can neither compose, endure, abandon, nor
escape, is unable to advance, unable to retreat, unable to stand
fixed. Nonetheless it stands under the impelling admonition to
move and resolve."[24] The need to pass through the barrier-with-
no-gate-that-is-myself + the nonexistence of God = the crisis of
the spiritual atheist. The possibility of a way out of this crisis, or
in the absence of a way out the possibility of living in the face of
it, must now be addressed.

PART 2

THE QUEST FOR ATHEISTIC SALVATION

IN PART ONE I tried to point to a problem inherent in human existence independent of gender, race, personal psychology, geographical locale, culture, or the era in which one lives. A problem that cannot be resolved politically, economically, historically, anthropologically, psychologically, or artistically.

This problem is encapsulated in Zen master Shin'ichi Hisamatsu's comment: "As long as 'I am,' as long as there is the ordinary self, there is disturbance."[25] In Richard DeMartino's: "It is not that the 'I' has a problem; the 'I' is the problem." In Paul Tillich's delineation of an anxiety, loneliness, insecurity, guilt, doubt, fear of death, and struggle with meaninglessness that, as he says, "belong to existence."

This problem is not an object, either in the world or in consciousness, but resides as the very awareness of consciousness and the world. As such it cannot be "attacked," since every move of the attacker further enacts the problem.

Martin Luther, Saint Augustine, Shinran, and others, intuiting this, located the sole possibility of the resolution to the problem of the "I" in some sort of divine "grace," either of Buddha or of God. The rejection of this grace and its divine sources makes me, and millions like me, an atheist. Among these millions, many have been forced by life into the conviction that the root of our suffering cannot be resolved by any human resource (such as thinking, feeling, or doing), and that some sort of transcendence of the "I" experience is required if the resolution is to be achieved. This conscripts us into the spiritual quest despite our atheism.

Yet virtually all the "seekers" of my generation that I know—despite years of struggle, including meditative struggle—do not feel much the freer. Perhaps what I have written will be of some use in our wondering why that is. A very great man, Ryūtarō Kitahara, concluded his beginning instructions on how to meditate with the line: "Try various ways of meditating, but when you are forced to confront what to do when all of them have failed—that is the essence of meditation." He died recently, and I dedicate what I have written to him.

11 EVADING IT

THE MOST COMMON way of contending with the intrinsic disquiet of being an "I" is to evade it. Most of us confront it only when its inner urgency forces us to. No one, even the heroic, confronts it all of the time. Heidegger wrote that for the most part it is dealt with by "an evasive turning away." Tillich wrote that "naked anxiety" cannot be endured for more than a few seconds. The saintly deaf-mute, Mr. Singer, in Carson McCullers's *The Heart Is a Lonely Hunter*, is fated to endure it perpetually, without a buffer, unprotected from the the silence of the infinite Void. It destroys him, despite the beauty of Mr. Singer's song that everyone can hear but him. In a heartbreaking scene in the film adaptation, one sees him at night seated in his chair, fingers pressed to his forehead in a vain effort to hold back the cascading abyss which gushes past his hand into the air of his boardinghouse room.

The tendency to place a buffer between oneself and the Void is as inveterate as the fear of death. "We run heedlessly into the abyss after putting something in front of us to stop us from seeing it," Pascal wrote in his *Pensées*. That "something" Pascal called human activity, which, he argued, could as a whole be placed in the category of diversion. Under the heading "activity" he writes this single sentence: "When a soldier complains of his hard life (or a laborer, etc.) try giving him nothing to do."[26] Each of us knows the difficulty of doing nothing. Each of us knows the difficulty of an empty apartment or room. Obviously the difficulty is not the room but the one—myself—who keeps the room from ever being empty. Stop busyness and vacuity pours through.

It may be as small as a pin prick in the chest. It may expand and swallow you. The abyss is frightening and the attempts to reduce it to manageable size are probably instinctive; a hole *in* me of whatever size is more capable of being dealt with than when the pin prick blows up and envelops me within the hole. Rarely do I wake in the morning without some gnawing sense of it. When standing on a street corner waiting for a traffic light to turn, if I examine my consciousness it lies in ambush, as if waiting for my recognition. All of us have had the experience of being attacked by it in the middle of a good time. Richard DeMartino calls it "the vacuousness of having fun," realized when the attempt to erase the Void through pleasure is undermined by vacuity.

The pin prick *is* the abyss in a compressed file. The void is not diminished when seemingly reduced in size. It expands and contracts of its own accord; in my case thirty-five years of meditation and frequent ecstatic meditation have not removed it; ecstatic meditation only *seems* to remove it. The ecstasy of meditation is in one profound sense the transformation of the "pain of loneliness" to the "glory of solitude," as Tillich would say, but under close scrutiny the pain is there even in the glory, ready to blow up in size again at any time. Mount Nothingness is hard to scale, each surmounting step drops one into a bog of Void. The attempt to flee from it is natural, despite poet Charles Olson's warning: "The hour of your flight will be the hour of your death."

This ambiguity Pascal saw as the basic contradiction of human experience. He wrote that while a "secret instinct" tells us that "the only true happiness lies in rest," a second instinct tells us:

Man finds nothing so intolerable as to be in a state of complete rest, without passions, without occupation, without diversion, without effort.

Then he faces his nullity, loneliness, inadequacy, dependence, helplessness, emptiness.

And at once there wells up from the depths of his soul boredom, gloom, depression, chagrin, resentment, despair.[27]

Pascal argued, essentially, that a janitor with a television to distract him would be far less wretched than a president without one, or some other effective means of repressing the abyss. A king "deprived of so-called diversion . . . is unhappy, indeed more unhappy than the humblest of his subjects who can enjoy sport and diversion."[28]

Put it to the test; leave a king entirely alone . . . with no one to keep him company and no diversion, with complete leisure to think about himself, and you will see that a king without diversion is a very wretched man. Therefore such a thing is carefully avoided, and the persons of kings are invariably attended by a great number of people concerned to see that diversion comes after affairs of state, watching over their leisure hours to provide pleasures and sport so that there should never be an empty moment.[29]

But the empty moment threatens to be *every* moment. "The fact is," Pascal wrote, "that the present usually hurts." He continued, "We are so unwise that we wander about in times that do not belong to us [the past and future]; and do not think of the only one that does; so vain that we dream of times that are not and blindly flee the only one that is . . . Thus we never actually live, but hope to live, and since we are always planning how to be happy, it is inevitable that we should never be so."[30] The sagely advice common to new age philosophy to "live in the now" overlooks that the now contains an element that is unendurable. That unendurable element spawns what Jiddu Krishnamurti called "the constant demand to be amused, to be entertained, to be taken away from ourselves." Failure to yield to this demand leads to boredom, the first symptom of the abyss. Beneath or within boredom lies loneliness: "the feeling of being utterly cut off, of suddenly being afraid without apparent cause. The mind knows this fear when for a moment it realizes that it can rely on nothing, that no distraction can take away the sense of self-enclosing emptiness."

Jiddu Krishnamurti says this in his illuminating talk "The Need to Be Alone." He asserts: "Very few go beyond this fear of loneliness, but one *must* go beyond it, because beyond it lies the real treasure." Sidestep this task and "you will find your whole life is nothing but an endless search for distractions." He adds, "If you run away . . . it will always be there waiting for you around the corner."[31]

I cite Pascal and Krishnamurti, one a westerner dead for hundreds of years, one an easterner of our own time, to suggest the universality of both the quest to deal with the abyss and the quest to evade it. Both the desire to flee it and the desire to dissolve it are born from the same root—the fact that, as Jiddu Krishnamurti says: "There is no human being who has not felt or will not feel that quivering anxiety." Loneliness is bottomless; when death threatens, no one fails to know that consciousness is ultimately lonely. As Heidegger says, the existence which is inevitably "mine" must be died, as it must be lived, by me alone. I once said to the Zen philosopher Masao Abe: "My whole life has been reduced to a battle between confrontation and evasion." He said: "There is no third thing. You need only to get to the bottom of that polarity." The polarity, like the abyss of loneliness, is itself bottomless, rendering the intent of most human activity ambiguous. Certainly Pascal, a tireless thinker and writer, knew the value of human effort, but he was honest enough to know that even the most creative activity expresses an evasive tendency as well. The best human doing, like the best human being, can be, as every artist and every lover experiences, double-edged—authentic and escapist. Remember Kafka's "There are countless hiding places, there is only one deliverance, but possibilities of deliverance are again as many as the hiding places."[32] When he wrote this Kafka told no lie. Nor when he wrote:

> He does not want consolation, but not because he does not want it—who does not want it?—but because

consolation means to devote one's whole life to this task, to live perpetually on the borders of one's existence and almost outside them, barely to remember for whom one is seeking consolation, and therefore not being able to find effective consolation (effective, not by any means real consolation, which does not exist).[33]

Evasion of the spiritual quest is of a spiritual root, driven by the attempt to contend with existential anxiety. But if neither real nor effective consolation exists, the tendency toward evasion must be fought off like a snarling dog.

12 CONFRONTING IT

1. CAUGHT IN THE VISE

I first heard about the possibility of "cosmic consciousness," of achieving oneness with the universe, when I was nineteen. For thirty-six years all other notions and possibilities have paled beside it. I have sought it, and evaded the search for it, in either case always defined by it. You can be deeply, fundamentally defined by something you try to evade.

Stated in other terms: finite, mortal existence longs for something not subject to the disappointment of the mortal and finite. This doesn't mean that this something exists. For the atheist that something as God *does* not exist.

A great part of the appeal of eastern thought is the prospect of the realization of the infinite, of oneself as infinite, without recourse to God. This I and my kind seek.

I see two motivations for this search. One might be called the back door: death, anxiety, insecurity, loneliness, the threat of there being no ultimate meaning, all snapping at your heels. The other might be called the front door: Forty years ago, a friend of mine saw the Wisconsin grain bending in the wind and glimpsed the infinite. The possibility of glimpsing it again has remained before him ever since at an unreachable distance—the front door.

Some spiritual atheists are shoved forward from the back, others pulled forward from the front. Eventually one finds oneself pressed in the vise of the two. Once pressed, it is hard to escape the double risk. The risk of dying without having realized one's ultimate aspiration; the risk, that is, of dying unfulfilled. And the risk of defining oneself by, and staking oneself on, an aspiration for something that is not real.

There are other risks. The composer Berlioz famously mocked: "*That* Chopin—he spent his whole life dying!" Is one a fool for being consumed with all that knocks at the back door, or a bigger fool for not hearing the pounding? I mentioned in Part One that the ascetic artiste Flaubert, during a Sunday visit watching a relative hang her wash, declared that she, not he, was "in the right." The equally ascetic Kafka never got over his love with that comment of Flaubert's and its sentiment that ordinary life and concerns were to be preferred over a life of isolated artistic genius. Even on his deathbed he sought the marriage he always sought to evade.

I remember a woman, very pregnant, during a discussion at a conference at a spiritual retreat center in New Mexico repeatedly asking: "Are there costs to the spiritual quest?" The sincerity of her concern—for herself, about what the quest would mean for the stability of her relationship with her partner (who was also in the room), for the fate of the child she was about to create—gave an anguished purity to her face. Several voices in the room blithely let her know that between the religious quest and the demands of domesticity there was no contradiction. When the session was over I walked over to Professor Richard DeMartino. His first words, under his breath, were: "Of course there are costs." This was consistent. Years before, when I'd made a glib remark about being free from the need for a relationship, he'd told me: "You pay the price either way."

2. PARADISE REFURBISHED

It is natural that the costs associated with the spiritual quest should be denied by these "seekers on the spiritual path" because in the last hundred years something profound has altered in our spiritual aspiration. Traditional conceptions of paradise were a synthesis of goodness and splendor. The Twenty-third Psalm, to take a celebrated example, united both. God "leadeth me beside the still waters" but he also "leadeth me in the path of righteousness." A heaven of virtue alone, without beauty, without splendor, would likely be hell. And yet one of the semi-conscious spiritual questions of our generation is whether the reverse could be true: Can't paradise be achieved without a great moral battle within oneself? Kierkegaard, in his book *Either/Or*, and elsewhere, distinguished in human spiritual life what he called the "aesthetic" stage—by which he means not only the search for beauty and pleasure but the pursuit of all heightened sensation—from the "ethical" stage. Paul Tillich emphasized that these are not so much stages as "tendencies" in all of us. The desire for exquisite experience at least equals, often trumps, the desire for good. This is made clear whenever we cause pain by choosing new love over the beloved to whom the words "I love you" were once spoken in commitment. Exquisite sensation, if we are honest, is often as important to us as any moral ideal. One consequence of the nonexistence of God is that the biblical "Thou shalt" is no longer binding, or at least no longer absolutely binding, even if one tries to resurrect it for oneself in secular or humanist or Kantian terms. For many atheists on the spiritual quest, the "Thou Shalt" that often pricks most is "Thou Shalt not die unfulfilled."

In my novel *The Atheists' Monastery* I tried to embody this drive for splendor at all costs in the character of the protagonist, Julius Cain, who seeks "heaven" at the expense of goodness, subordinating men, women, and morality to his search for personal fulfillment. He is a man spiritually driven by his need to break free of all that negates him—whether the pain of unfulfilled desire, the tedium of desire fulfilled, the artistic masterpieces he creates but which disappoint him, or death—ever longing, despite the impossibility of faith, for something beyond the finite, mortal character that spoils all his experience. Though capable of awful things he is not a bad man. He has intuited that neither ethics nor repentance is requisite for the realization of cosmic consciousness or Oneness. And this is a central, if again semiconscious, insight of our times.

Not that anyone intentionally disregards the good. Among spiritual atheists I have seen a genuine longing to be loving and compassionate, but with a minimum of moral struggle. Enlightenment is conceived (I recognize this in myself) as a kind of "big bang" whose natural by-product will be a compassionate, loving heart. There is a certain great sense to this: one often hurts others out of one's own pain and incompleteness; and the eternal delight which is the concomitant of enlightenment, the texts and the masters promise, will provide a completeness that puts an end to all need. Non-dual with the universe, one is all, one needs nothing, so why hurt others? Appealing, is it not?

In sum: even if God has been evicted, still "his house has many mansions" but paradise has been redecorated and virtue, for many aspirants, no longer occupies a front room. While I lived in Japan I met many westerners—author included—interested in Zen, in Buddhism, in Hindu mysticism and Taoism. I never met one with a genuine existential interest in Confucianism. Of course, Confucianism is often odious with its oppressive hierarchies among social relations, but that alone does not account for western indifference. Buddhism, Taoism, and Hinduism too have their odious social elements. But they also promise the delight of the big bang of cosmic splendor that Confucianism does not. Seekers of enlightenment are far more willing to struggle for splendor than for good. They will endure hours of pain in meditation, of deprived sleep, of cold. I have watched this during grueling meditation retreats. But there has been a shift. Beauty has been separated from goodness in much contemporary western spiritual aspiration.

This shift, and I think there is no way of getting around its implications, corresponds to the atheistic interest in the religions of self-awakening as opposed to the religions of faith. The poetry of the Zen masters almost always expresses enlightenment in aesthetic terms, almost never invoking the ethical. One reads in these poems of the sound of the rain dripping from the eaves, of the splendor of the moon, not of virtuous deeds. There is deep reason for this. Ask yourself what has been the greatest moment of your life and see if it is one of splendor and exquisite well-being, or one of ethical goodness. Or ask yourself what *would be* the greatest moment of your life, and note whether it occupies the aesthetic or the ethical domain. Dostoyevsky, in *The Idiot*, describes Prince Myshkin's moment of ecstasy and harmony as worth giving up the whole of one's life for. If one reaches a moment of sufficient intensity of beauty, that moment alone can be the meaning of life. Those who know this cannot help longing for its onset or its repetition, or (at the center of what we often conceive of as enlightenment) its permanence.

Enlightenment, in a way that cannot be repressed (nor perhaps should it be), comes to be sought as the endpoint of Freud's pleasure principle: enlightenment as a pleasure of eternal duration. (A possibility Freud would have denied; for him intense pleasure was by necessity sporadic.) Television advertising has glimpsed the way in which desire and ultimate human aspiration unite in the "aesthetic" domain: never is a product sold because it will bring virtue; many are sold promising splendor. Consider the beer commercial depicting the "perfect moment," tasted among friends in snowcapped mountains or among beautiful people frolicking on a beach with the tagline: "This is as good as it gets." The standard of "goodness" becomes the quality of sensation, and not only in the West. When I lived in Japan, smoking cigarettes was advertised as the cap to the perfect moment; a frequent radio ad on a prominent jazz program described listening to Miles Davis at some New York club—the click of the lighter, the inhalation and exhalation, marking the summit of lived life.

Intoxication with life, life overflowing with life, life permanently broken free from humdrum routine, sublime experience as the goal and purpose of life—all of us understand the appeal. It is encapsulated in Byron's lines: "The great object of life is Sensation—to feel that we exist . . . It is this 'craving void' which drives us to gaming—to battle, to travel—to intemperate but keenly felt pursuits of any description."[34] The craving for heightened existence through heightened sensation is central to the story of the search for enlightenment in much of this generation of spiritual atheists. We seek Cosmic Splendor, relieved that there is no Divine Law.

3. THE CONTRADICTION BETWEEN THE IMPOSSIBILITY OF A WAY TO LIBERATION—AND THE NEED FOR A WAY TO LIBERATION—AS THE ONLY "WAY"

"Confronting it" implies something to be confronted and a means of confronting—a path or way, a "how to." The seeker seeks a method. But the nature of the problem of being human implies that there can be no path, no "how to" in the ordinary sense of the term, not even that of meditation. Paul Tillich's comment, "The situation of existence cannot be overcome in the power of this situation. Every attempt to do so strengthens this situation, which can be summed up in the title of Sartre's play, *No Exit*," expresses not only the problem of human existence but the contradiction in every effort to resolve it.

Yet the impossibility of a way does nothing to diminish the necessity of a way, since no one has the luxury to live and die without a solution even if all attempts fail. Impaled on the contradiction that there is no way, yet there must be a way—a "way" emerges. *The only method is the deepening of the contradiction between the need for a "how to" and the absence of one.*

4. THE AMBIGUOUS CALM OF MEDITATION

Meditation is one of the primary vehicles to glimpses of splendor. I am a meditation junkie. I meditate four to six hours per day in one posture or another. The number of days I have not meditated in the last thirty-five years would not total a month. If I wake in the middle of the night I often sit for two to four hours until I need to sleep again. The most exquisite experiences of my life have been in meditation. While hiking up a mountain in Switzerland several years ago, the pain in my sinus area caused by exertion in high altitude gave way to an intense surge of pleasurable energy; since that day I often am able to approach the state achieved during sitting meditation while I'm walking. Meditation stuffs my brain with the full moon. It gives me ecstasy, has brought me through illness and emotional turmoil.

Countless atheists discipline themselves in meditation without adherence or attachment to any religious doctrine or system. Many of us do so in the anticipation of experience released from the conflict and aridity of ordinary life. This promise of an experience transcendent to common human experience makes meditation a great source of hope. Most meditators practice each day with that hope, and most probably have moments which justify it. The Zen master Shin'ichi Hisamatsu remarked that no pleasure surpassed the pleasure of meditation. For me its beauties exceed the mountains of Norway or the most beautiful music and art. Nothing else I know so transforms the pain of loneliness into the glory of solitude.

Mêng-shan writes: "I was as pure and transparent as a snow-filled silver bowl or as the autumnal sky cleared of all darkening clouds . . . My mental condition then was like the reflection of the moon penetrating the depths of a running stream the surface of which was in rapid motion, while the moon retained its perfect shape and serenity despite the commotion of the water." Hsueh Yen writes: "I came to realize a state in which the dualism of body and mind ceased to exist. I felt so transparent and lively that my eyelids were kept open all the time." T'ien-shan Ch'iung records: "On the second day I could not close my eyelids even if I wanted to; on the third day I felt as if I were walking on air; and on the fourth day all worldly affairs ceased to bother me. That night I was leaning against the railing for a while, and when I examined myself I found that the field of consciousness seemed to be all empty . . . One day I began my zazen [meditation] at four in the afternoon and continued until four in the morning, and through sheer power of concentration I reached an exquisite state of ecstasy."[35] A Japanese monk friend says: "The texts call it 'emptiness.' But it is really joy."

Yet T'ien-shan Ch'iung continues: "Coming out of it I saw the master [Mêng-shan] and told him about it. He then asked: 'What is your original self?' I was about to speak when he shut the door in my face."

Why?

Consider this troubling quotation from a talk by Jiddu Krishnamurti:

Meditation is not conscious meditation. What we have been taught is conscious, deliberate meditation, sitting cross-legged or lying down or repeating certain phrases, which is a deliberate, conscious effort to meditate. The speaker says such meditation is nonsense. It is part of desire. Desiring to have a peaceful mind is the same as desiring a good house or a good dress. Conscious meditation destroys, prevents the other form of meditation.[36]

The serenity of what Krishnamurti calls "conscious meditation" is ambiguous. The joy of meditation can drive one to the complacency of delight in what Hermann Hesse called, in his novel *Siddhartha,* a "well-upholstered hell." The Zen master Po-shan warned of the addictive power that overcomes those who have once tasted the "honeyed-sweetness" of meditative ecstasy. The pain, banished, only seemingly vanishes. It is the jack-in-the-box within meditative beauty. The pain of the "I" is not an object *within* consciousness but human consciousness itself. As such no transient alteration of consciousness can eradicate the root of suffering. Despite its obvious blessings, meditation rarely shatters this root; failing to do so it is subject to the limitations of any intoxicant or high. Call to mind Siddhartha's remarks to his friend Govinda after years of mastery of asceticism and meditative practice:

Siddhartha said: "What I have learned from the samanas [ascetics] . . . I could have learned more quickly and more simply. I could have learned it in any tavern in a prostitutes' district, my friend, among the teamsters and dice players."

Govinda said: "Siddhartha is joking with me. How could you have learned concentration [meditation] . . . among those miserable creatures?"

And Siddhartha said softly, as if speaking to himself: "What is concentration? What is the ability to leave one's body? What is fasting? What is retention of breath? It is a flight from the self, it is a brief escape from the torment of being 'I,' it is a numbing of the mind to counter pain and the senselessness of life. The same escape, the same brief numbing, is found by the ox drover in his inn when he drinks a few bowls of rice wine or fermented coconut milk. Then he no longer feels his self, then he no longer feels the pains of life, then he finds a brief numbing of the mind. When he has dosed off over his bowl of rice wine, he finds the same thing Siddhartha and Govinda find when, in lengthy exercises, they are released from their bodies and dwell in the nonself. It is thus, O Govinda."

Govinda said: "You speak thus, O friend, and yet you know that Siddhartha is no drover and a samana is not a drunkard. Yes, the drinker is numbed for a while; yes, he finds a brief escape and rest, but he comes out of his delusion and finds that everything is still the same; he has not grown wiser, he has not gathered knowledge, he has not risen a few steps higher."

And Siddhartha said with a smile: "I do not know. I have never been a drinker. But that I, Siddhartha, find only a brief numbing in my exercises and bouts of concentration, and that I am just as far removed from wisdom and salvation as a child in the womb: this I know, O Govinda, this I know."[37]

For this reason Richard DeMartino calls meditation a "local anesthetic." It can easily fall prey to Pascal's charge of evasion.

In P. D. Ouspensky's *In Search of the Miraculous,* his teacher Gurdjieff emphasizes the necessity of breaking out of prison. Hesse's "well-upholstered hell" points to the importance of not confusing decorating one's prison with breaking out. Consider this exchange with the greatest Hindu of the twentieth century, Ramana Maharshi:

> QUESTIONER: I arrive at a stage of stillness of mind beyond which I find myself unable to proceed further. I have no thought of any kind and there is an emptiness, a blankness. A mild light pervades and I feel bodiless . . . The experience lasts nearly half an hour and is pleasing. Would I be correct in concluding that all that was necessary to secure eternal happiness, that is, freedom or salvation or whatever one calls it, was to continue the practice till this experience could be maintained for hours, days, and months together?
>
> RAMANA MAHARSHI: This does not mean salvation. Such a condition is termed *manolaya* or temporary stillness of thought. *Manolaya* means concentration, temporarily arresting the movements of thoughts. As soon as the concentration ceases, thoughts, old and new, rush in as usual; and even if this temporary lulling of mind should last a thousand years, it will never lead to . . . liberation from birth and death. The practitioner must therefore be ever on the alert and inquire within as to who has this experience, who realizes its pleasantness.

Without this enquiry he will go into a long trance or a deep sleep [yoga nidra]. Due to the absence of a proper guide at this stage of spiritual practice, many have been deluded and fallen prey to a false sense of liberation and only a few have managed to reach the goal safely . . . In *manolaya* there is a temporary subsidence of thought waves, and though the temporary period may last for a thousand years, thoughts, which are thus temporarily stilled, rise up as soon as the *manolaya* ceases.[38]

Millions meditate; few are liberated. "Yes," one may say, "because few take meditation to its ultimate, liberating depths." This is obviously true, but not simply on account of a lack of meditative skill, or effort. The famous anecdote where Huai-jang disturbs Ma-tsu's meditation by trying to polish a brick into a mirror has the bemused Ma-tsu chide: "How can you hope to polish a piece of brick into a mirror?" Huai-jang fires back: "How can you sit yourself into a Buddha? . . . If the ox cart does not move, do you whip the cart or do you whip the ox?" Meditation "whips" the cart. The whipper/meditator generally emerges untouched.

Ramana Maharshi makes the distinction between the bucket (ego) submerged in the well (submerged in *Brahman*, in the "One"), yet still fastened to its rope, and the bucket severed from the rope. It is the distinction between *samadhi*—as generally understood as the temporary ecstatic overcoming of duality—and

enlightenment or liberation. The exquisite pleasure of *samadhi*—
with all its wonderful benefits—usually does not transform in any
ultimate sense of the term, despite the proneness of meditators to
declare their meditation as transformative. The ecstasy of meditation, both in my experience and in my observation of other
meditators, usually changes little in the fundamental depths of a
person. Psychologist-meditators such as Jeffrey Rubin are now
writing of patients who have the same personal and interpersonal
problems they had years before despite decades of meditation.
He sees this, in part, as a consequence of the "letting go" that
meditation gurus so frequently recommend. What is required, he
suggests, is not merely a letting go of, but a confrontation with,
psychological problems. This is a profound point. I would argue,
however, that the primary reason liberation does not occur is not
that meditation leaves neuroses unresolved but that in almost all
cases meditation leaves the rope uncut. The problematic self is
plunged in the ecstasy of the "well" temporarily, leaving the "on-
tological" or existential structure which makes the self a problem
intact. The basic existential anxiety of being human consequently
remains, whatever the other benefits of meditative calm.

The desire to quell that anxiety by losing oneself in the
hard-earned, well-deserved joys of meditation is as natural
as the instinct for self-preservation. The ambiguous tension
between the desire for both ego maintenance and ego loss, a

permanent feature of the spiritual quest, pervades meditation as well. A friend astutely observes that most of the westerners interested in Zen that he has known, whatever they might claim, are looking for an enriched ego-existence rather than liberation *from* the ego, the usual meaning of liberation in eastern religion. The obvious retort is: "So what's wrong with that?" Nothing, if one honestly can say: "Nothing!"

The actual value of meditation will far more often consist in beautifying the prison rather than in the prison break. In creating a sanctuary within the intrinsically estranged condition of being a self rather than the breaking through of the fettering conditions. In permitting an intermittent, if fabulous, bite from the tree of life that does not end exile from paradise.

5. THE "OTHER" MEDITATION

"Conscious meditation destroys, prevents the other form of meditation," wrote Jiddu Krishnamurti. This other form of meditation I will try to explore. Two riddles to begin with:

> Zazen [sitting meditation] was the one way out. But it too is a waste. And yet I can't stop sitting. In the failure of zazen, the best zazen—the path of escape, the opening— disappears. Zazen at its best fails, and this brings into greater clarity that there's no way out. Zazen should be the one means of escape, and when you can take it no

further and it still leaves the problem unsolved you are thrown back into daily life with the problem pressing in ever more intensively. *(From a 1986 New Year's Eve conversation with Kenzō Toyoshima, the one person I know who meditates at the risk of his life.)*

BERNARD PHILLIPS: If you follow any way, you will never get there.
SHIN'ICHI HISAMATSU: That is correct.
BERNARD PHILLIPS: And if you do not follow any way, you will never get there.
SHIN'ICHI HISAMATSU: That is correct.
BERNARD PHILLIPS: So one faces a dilemma.
SHIN'ICHI HISAMATSU: Let that dilemma be your way! [i.e., it is that very dilemma that is the way you must follow!][39]

Which brings me to Hisamatsu.

6. SHIN'ICHI HISAMATSU'S RELIGIOUS ATHEISM

Standing will not do, nor will sitting. Feeling will not do, nor will thinking. Dying will not do, nor will living. Then, what do you do? Here is the ultimate, single barrier by means of which if one is pressed to the extremity, there is a transformation, and where there is a transformation, the "I"-barrier is passed through.

—Shin'ichi Hisamatsu

Shin'ichi Hisamatsu (1889–1980) was a Zen master—a civilian, not a monk—who made it quite clear that Zen did not need Buddhism, nor did it need Zen. One of his deathbed calligraphies reads: "My final utterance—Killing Buddha, killing God." In his essay *Atheism*, Hisamatsu writes:

> The words of Nietzsche: "God is dead," . . . must be the true cry of the modern person. I also cannot suppress my profound agreement with these words. The phrase "I am Godless" well expresses the self-awareness of the modern human being. "Christianity is a stain on man which cannot be wiped away" is by no means simply some bombastic utterance of Nietzsche. It is a cry from the heart and mind of modern humanity.[40]

For Hisamatsu, atheism is an indispensable element of the autonomy of self that defines the modern age. The saving power of God or of a deified Buddha, even if it existed, would be an unacceptable violation and forfeiture of human freedom. "To be a person of faith is not the true way of being a human person."[41] Faith must be negated if true personhood is to be achieved. "The kind of religion which has been negated by modernity has today no longer any need for continued existence, nor is there any room for it."[42]

Yet Hisamatsu holds that modernity not only negates God, it negates the human being. We must rid ourselves of God, but the resulting "homocentrism" in which freedom, happiness, and peace are sought through human power alone brings none of these. The primary supposition of homocentrism, that human existence is able to sustain itself by its own power, is a lie. Every honest life discovers what Hisamatsu calls the "moment"—the moment wherein it is understood that one is prevented, by virtue of being human, from ever being at ease. Human existence is subverted by human existence. Hisamatsu calls this "the fundamental crisis of human nature," the "deadlock of human autonomy." We are forced to rely on a self-power that drowns us. The human person is "atheistic, and yet utterly unable to rest in human-absolutism. Nonetheless, it cannot give up its atheism."[43] He continues, "If we delve further, will it not be seen that human nature is essentially atheistic and, moreover, human-negating? It can be said that in the present era, this fact has come to appear. In other words, this is a human-negating era and a God-negating era."[44]

For Hisamatsu, the predicament of the "I," along with its powerlessness to resolve that predicament by any human recourse, makes religion imperative. But God does not, and cannot, exist. "Self-power" and "other-power" both are of no avail. Yet the demand in each of us that a resolution be achieved cannot be erased. This means that the "religious imperative" can be met, in Hisamatsu's view, only by surmounting the homocentric position without recourse to theism.

Therefore, religion from here on, while a-theonomous [without God], must negate the ordinary way of being human as well . . . Religion cannot simply let the human person remain as human person, and yet it will not do if religion is theism. Consequently, it must be an *atheistic religion*.[45]

7. HISAMATSU'S FUNDAMENTAL KOAN

The negation of all human and divine resources, and the consequent necessity to crush the power of this negation, Hisamatsu expressed through what he called the fundamental koan: "When whatever you do will not do, what do you do?" The Japanese phrase, *doshitemo ikenakereba do suru ka*, could as well be translated: "When whatever you are will not do, what do you do?" for the human problem comprises being as well as doing. He insisted that this koan is not one koan among others, but the essence of all koan. Its significance is to have built the Great Wall of China into every teacup, every flower, every movement of the world, as can be seen in his encounter with Ryūtarō Kitahara (1922–2004), who recorded the following account:

The night before [Hisamatsu's] talk I escorted him, in the snow, back to his dwelling . . . Entering, I was served powdered green tea. But when I had been sipping it for half a minute or so, Dr. Hisamatsu suddenly scolded: "Drink it without using your mouth." Cornered, I dashed the tea in my face. He said, "No good," with a scowl, and then, extending his hand, charged: "Pass that teacup without using your hands . . . Take this plate without using your hands." I was utterly at a loss, but Dr. Hisamatsu pressed me: "Sitting will not do; what do you do? . . . You can do anything—stand up!" Standing, I was told: "Standing will not do, what do you do?" Then when I'd assumed a crouching position: "Remaining motionless will not do, what do you do? . . . As you are, leave!" When I'd descended from the verandah, I was bombarded with, "Return without walking!"[46]

This passage discloses the manner in which the root or "universal" or "total" negation embedded in Hisamatsu's fundamental koan (and in human existence) is nothing abstract, but entails at once the particular negation—or repudiation—of every specific thought, feeling, or act. Sitting will not do when one sits; standing will not do if one stands. The negation (or repudiation) of a particular gesture is, conversely, always the universal negation of all gestures. Sitting will not do when one sits already includes standing will not do if one stands. This is made clear in a commentary of Hisamatsu on a renowned Zen koan:

In ninth-century China there lived a famous Zen master, Xiangyan Zhixian [Hsiang-yen Chih-hsien], who said: "If on the way you meet an accomplished man, greet him with neither speech nor silence." Xiangyan meant that in meeting a person who has attained awakening or nirvana, neither speech nor silence will do. How, then, should we greet an awakened person? This question must . . . be considered to imply a total, ultimate problem in it, and not anything particular, such as having recourse to words or keeping silent.[47]

It is never the case that sitting will not do but standing will. The radical insufficiency of sitting entails the powerlessness of all human acts, including remaining motionless, to break free of the contradiction that every self is. The failure of any particular thought, feeling, or deed is immediately the failure of all undertakings, *insofar as the aim of those undertakings is the ultimate solution of the ultimate human problem.* (Great painting, as Michelangelo knew, makes one a great painter but does not make one free.) Similarly, just as the koan "Sitting will not do; what do you do?," "Standing will not do, what do you do?," and "Remaining motionless will not do, what do you do?" are particular applications of the universal koan, "When whatever you do (or are) will not do, what do you do?," so Hisamatsu's injunctions to Kitahara, "Drink the tea without using your mouth," "Pass that teacup without using your hands," and "Take this plate without using your hands," are concrete applications of another form of fundamental koan

Hisamatsu was known to employ. Namely: "Without using your mouth, without using your mind, without using your body, express yourself!" In both koan the same structure is evident. "Whatever you do will not do" and "Without using your mouth, without using your mind, without using your body" both point to the powerlessness of all human thinking, feeling, doing, and being to procure ultimate freedom, happiness, or peace. Both place a demand on us: I *must* be released from my discontent; I must find peace. No realization of insufficiency or failure can rid us of this demand. It is an impossible demand (for the unawakened), with both the impossibility and the demand existentially binding and ineradicable. Drink tea in an attempt to resolve one's fundamental estrangement and the mouth is negated; pass a teacup—or paint a masterpiece—and the hands are stripped away. And again, in the stripping away of the mouth or hands, all else is stripped away. All but the imperative to resolve.

These koan thus form an unalterable equation. One side of the equation negates us totally, the other demands unconditionally. One side of the equation shows the impossibility of finding a solution to the problem of being a self, the other shows the necessity of resolution despite the impossibility. This contradiction (or tension) is the core of Hisamatsu's koan. But as Richard DeMartino's distinction between the "natural koan" and the koan "given by a master" I hope has made clear,[48] the koan given from the outside has no authority except as a mirror, as an external formulation of our own inevitable inner struggle. A koan is capable of this deprivation, or negation, only because it is simultaneously an expression of the problematic way of being of persons. It renders impotent every resource utilized to deliver human persons from their affliction only because every resource is in fact impotent to do so.

The right side of the koan equation—"What do you do?" or "Express yourself!"—reflects the demand for transcendence. If no amount of success can satisfy the demand, no amount of failure can erase the demand. No government can erase it. We ourselves cannot erase it. Nor can the nonexistence of God.

It is in this sense that Hisamatsu, a radical atheist, is a religious man. By religion Hisamatsu means but two things: first, the impulse or longing for self-transcendence which arises with the realization that human nature will not do; second, the actual, living solution to the dilemma that plagues every self that lives. But again, neither the urgency nor difficulty of contending with this dilemma obviates that for Hisamatsu "religion from here on in . . . must be an *atheistic religion*." He has no vested interest in any specific religion, including Zen, which while a historical manifestation of a spiritual atheism is but one of its possibilities.

8. THE STRIPPING AWAY OF EVERY WAY AS THE WAY OUT

In a 1958 conversation with Paul Tillich, Hisamatsu observes that the reason most people live and die without finding a solution to the problem of being an "I" is "attributable to the fact that there can be no resolution to the religious problem until [the problem] first becomes fully—or unconditionally, activated in the person. Unfortunately, this consummation is generally not achieved, even though it ought to be."[49] These drab lines hide a razor in them: the solution to the problem is possible only when the problem is intensified to its ultimate, agonizing extent. In Zen parlance: "If you don't enter the tiger's cave you cannot snare the tiger's cub." In Hesse's novel *Siddhartha*: "Everything that was not suffered to the end and finally concluded, recurred." In Kafka's terms: "There is a point of no return. That point must be reached."

It is rarely reached, even by meditation. Why? Hisamatsu writes:

> If, when sitting, sitting is no good, what do you do? If, when standing, standing is no good, what do you do? When our sitting is no good, perhaps we stand. When standing is unacceptable, we probably walk. When walking is no good, we run. Or we say something, ask something, or eat something. If we continue in this way, no matter how much we are told [or tell ourselves] that our action is of no avail, there is always some kind of way out.[50]

This is the dilemma of false escape by a lateral movement. If "the present usually hurts," as Pascal said, and if no *now* can divest itself of the lack that makes it impossible to say, as Faust could not say, "Stay! Thou art so beautiful," it is natural to sidestep the inadequacy of each act by moving on to the next. Our ability to do so means "there is always some kind of way out," preventing us from finding a true way out. This accounts for the failure of Josef K. in Kafka's *The Trial*. Though under arrest, he is told by the interrogating officer he is "free to go to the bank"—by implication, free to do anything else: free in the sense Martin Luther meant in saying men and women are free to do everything but to free themselves of their bondage. To be freed from bondage the bondage must be made total. This necessitates that the ostensible way out via the next act be closed off. This is the symbolic significance of the bodhi tree, seat of Siddhartha Gautama's enlightenment. He does not sit there as an act of will but because he can go no further as an "I." Says Hisamatsu:

> When I am charged with, "Sitting will not do! What do you do?"—because it is I, after all, who am thus pressed, if sitting will not do, I stand. Herein, "Sitting will not do! What do you do?" applies only to the act of sitting. But when "sitting won't do!" includes the totality of all possible actions, then we arrive at a situation of ultimate extremity. Where "Sitting will not do!

What do you do?" opens out into the realization that
the totality of all possible situations will not do, then
standing as well is no longer possible. We can neither
sit nor stand. What can we possibly do then? We are
thrust into a total, existential dilemma. If we truly come
to be thus thoroughly cornered, this dilemma is broken
through and a new functioning emerges. If, however,
we are not truly cornered, this new functioning will not
appear. When, whether walking, standing, sitting, or
lying, all routes of mind [and body] are cut off such that
we are brought to the extremity, the breakthrough and
the new functioning will occur. If we truly penetrate the
existential koan of "Cornered, one passes through" . . .
we can, at a single stroke, "awaken to the true Self."[51]

To achieve this cornering is the cross without Christ. It
has its theological correlate in the phrase: "Man's extremity is
God's opportunity." Ancient China, through the I Ching, offers
its atheistic analogue: "When pressed to the extremity there is a
change, where there is a change there is a passing through." The
cornering is mandatory, and harrowing. Anyone who attempts
to activate it will know hell. Thus the Hindu mystic Ramakrishna
had his first breakthrough at the moment of attempted suicide
and his second when his guru stabbed a piece of glass between
his eyes. Thus Ramana Maharshi broke through at age seven-
teen, overpowered by the certitude of imminent death. Thus
Bankei Yōtaku, on the verge of death from consumption, broke

through upon spitting black phlegm against the wall, curing his illness at the same instant. Since there is no path to it, requiring instead the stripping away of all paths, it cannot be gained by a straight line. I take this as the meaning of Jiddu Krishnamurti's famous 1928 dictum: "Truth is a pathless land." Chuang Tzu wrote: "Only when there is no path and no procedure can you get to the Way."[52] Richard DeMartino insisted that the duality between path and goal could not be overcome dualistically—by following a path toward an end. Kafka likewise understood that every path was too late: "There is a goal but no way; what we call a way is hesitation."

U. G. Krishnamurti (the "other" Krishnamurti) explains in the most detail:

> There is no jnana marga [path of wisdom]. There is no marga [path] at all. It is total surrender—throwing in the towel, throwing in the sponge—and what comes out is jnana [wisdom]. It is not surrender in the ordinary sense of the word. It means there isn't anything you can do. That is total surrender, total helplessness. It can't be brought about through any effort or volition of yours. If you want to surrender to something, it's only to get something. That's why I use the words "a state of total surrender." It's a state of surrender where all effort has come to an end, where all movement in the direction of getting something has come to an end. . . .

It is very difficult for you to understand the absurdity of the whole of sadhana [spiritual practice]. (I am blocking every escape as it were. Even that outlet has to be blocked to put you in a corner. You must be choked to death, as it were.) . . . Whatever you are doing is blocking its happening . . . Whatever you are doing in any direction is only strengthening or distorting the whole thing.[53]

Again, since the barrier is not an object, but he or she who seeks to pass through the barrier, any move the barrier makes perpetuates the problem one seeks to resolve. What is required is the erasure of every path so that I am without further move. Hisamatsu is no less iron-fisted:

[Master Wu-men Hui-k'ai (Mumon Ekai in Japanese, 1183–1260) remarks:] "If one is to attain the wondrous awakening, it is necessary for the routes of the mind to be brought to the extremity and then extinguished." This is critically important. The [Japanese] compound *shinro* means "the routes of the mind." All the variously generated routes of the mind must be brought to the extremity and completely extinguished so that not one remains. The phrase in Wu-men's commentary reads "routes of the mind," but this is not necessarily to be restricted simply to the mind as separated from the body. All routes, inner and outer, are to be brought to the extremity and then utterly extinguished. This is crucial.[54]

When every recourse and resource by which the "I" maintains itself are expended, it collapses. But as Richard DeMartino expressed it in *Zen Buddhism and Psychoanalysis*: "the negative dissolution is at once a positive resolution."[55] The phoenix—what Hisamatsu calls "the Self without life-and-death living in the midst of life-and-death"—soars out of its own ashes. But I'm getting ahead of myself.

9. MEDITATION AS NOT BEING ABLE TO EVADE THE PROBLEM, EVEN THROUGH MEDITATION

How to arrive at a goal that has no way, and can be reached only with the elimination of all ways, is, I believe, what Jiddu Krishnamurti means by "the other form of meditation," the meditation that the meditation millions of us practice prevents or destroys. A statement by Jiddu Krishnamurti quoted in Mary Lutyen's abridgment of her original three-volume biography of him gives a clue as to what this other form of meditation might be:

> We are seeing the fact, the "what is," which is suffering . . . I suffer and the mind is doing everything it can to run away from it . . . So don't escape from sorrow, which does not mean that you become morbid. Live with it . . . What takes place? Watch. The mind is very clear, sharp. It is faced with the fact. The very suffering

transformed into passion is enormous. From that arises
a mind that could never be hurt. Full stop. That is the
secret.[56]

That he does not mean watching in the ordinary sense,
wherein there is a distinction between the watching-observer
and the suffering-watched, Krishnamurti also makes clear:

> What is sorrow? Is sorrow self-pity? Please investigate.
> We are not saying it is or it is not . . . Is sorrow brought
> about by loneliness—feeling desperately alone, iso-
> lated? . . . Can we look at sorrow as it actually is in us,
> and remain with it, hold it, and not move away from
> it? Sorrow is not different from the one who suffers.
> The person who suffers wants to run away, escape, do
> all kinds of things . . . [N]ever escape from it—then you
> will see for yourself, if you really look deeply, that there
> is an end to sorrow.[57]

In the "other" meditation, consciousness must focus on itself
in such a way that it is pulled into its own wound—at its root,
which is the root of itself as a self. DeMartino wrote much the
same in a letter to me while I was living in Kyoto: "Focus on the
root-source of the problem (or motivation) that made you go to
Japan. Let the restlessness and untenability of this problem (or
motivation)—at its source—be the motivating power and direct-
ing force of your quest." This is not to be achieved through an

act or technique of concentration, but only when one is grasped by the wound—the restlessness, the "natural koan" that I am—in such a way that the wound can no longer be converted into an object of consciousness. In ordinary concentration, awareness of the wound can be let go; in the "other" meditation the wound will not let go no matter how one tries to relinquish it. This is difficult to achieve because human consciousness by its very structure keeps slipping out of the wound, distancing itself from it, turning it into an object. So long as that occurs the suffering will not be brought to an end. In the words of Richard DeMartino:

> The ego has . . . to actualize the problematic of itself and its being in terms of the basic root or core contradiction, and not keep functioning in that contradiction as an ever-regressing subject. In other words, the ego is always stepping outside of its contradiction, though it is never outside, but only seeming to step outside of it. This regression has to be blocked. The ego as an ever-regressing subject must be blocked so that it cannot keep on in this unending regress. Therefore, the initial or provisional aim . . . is to stop this regressing subject from continually moving back, and block it so that it can't go back any more and is forced somehow to try to get into this contradiction in and of itself. To actualize this problematic in and of itself. . .

How does one get into—or actualize oneself as—the koan or problem? Well, you keep working on it but finally . . . to use Tillich's terms, it has to grasp the ego, but in such a way that the duality between ego and koan (or problem) is overcome. Insofar as one "works *on*" a koan, one will never solve the koan. Insofar as one "concentrates *on*" a koan, one will never solve the koan, the problem. Insofar as one "meditates *on*" a koan, one is never going to solve the problem.

So, insofar as the problem is outside the ego as an object, it is never going to be solved. On the other hand, this ever-regressing nature of the subject always turns it into an object. That's the problem. How do you overcome it? I'm suggesting, nothing the ego can do can overcome it. Because what has to be overcome is precisely that duality between this objectified koan (or problem) and the ego . . . You can't get around the dilemma. You can't get around the contradiction. You can't get around the anguish in that sense.

There's nothing the ego can do. And yet, as Dr. Phillips said [in the previously quoted Phillips–Hisamatsu exchange], if the ego doesn't do anything, it [the resolution] is not going to happen either. And so, Dr. Hisamatsu's statement remains: "That dilemma is the way you must follow."

Now, you say, "How do you do that?" Well, the minute you ask that question, obviously, you're not following the dilemma.[58]

"All you can do is keep your nose to the grindstone," DeMartino once said. "On the other hand, the nose *is* the grindstone."

10. LASHED TO THE MAST

To repeat: if the barrier is the one seeking to ram through the barrier, then one is blocked at the first move. For this reason alone do I lash myself each night to the mast of consciousness. From 9 PM until morning I alternate between meditation and sleep. On my back, on cushions, in a chair, on my feet, I seek to have the gravity of the wound pull me in. The wound lurks in ambush as I mount the meditation cushions and cross my legs or stretch across my bed. It stabs me in the pit of the stomach like a thrust harpoon. Too often—for a moment—I turn on the radio by my cushions to postpone the onset of awareness. Sometimes the wound cannot be located; clouded over, or by the residual beauty of previous meditation, for a time obscured. But only for a time. The wound is the default mode of consciousness. Not an object, but the awareness of every object; it will have its say. In her journal, Sylvia Plath writes: "the loneliness of the soul in its appalling self-consciousness is horrible and overpowering."[59]

Everything rests on entering the source of the wound, which is consciousness, so totally that even the awareness of the wound is transcended. In DeMartino's terms: "One must no longer simply be the bearer of the wound but be the wound itself." To do so defies method or technique, and for that reason requires none. One need not be an adept meditator in the ordinary sense. DeMartino, always adamant that genuine meditation had nothing to do with a specific body position, very early on said to me: "Sit in a chair, confront the problem an hour a day and take it from there."

The "method," insofar as one can speak of method, consists simply in *not running* from the contradiction that there is no way to resolve one's disquiet—but that there must be. Since the running is not merely intentional, but derives from the deepest drive of consciousness to distance itself from the pain that it is, this is a war. Seek the source of the wound—it proves ever receding, since it is not an object. The seeker is forced to inch after it in pursuit. In the recesses of the mind an energized beauty appears. Energized sufficiently, the beauty turns ecstatic.

Little excels the thrill of these ecstatic states. The gorgeousness of the mind. The mind an expanse of white frost. The mind brightest silk. Consciousness bathed in milk. The vibrancy of repose. The tapping into pure health. Clear, cold ice suffusing the clarified field of awareness. Mind burned away like a cigarette pressed into the center of a leaf—little excels it. The question of what to do next against the incontrovertible knowledge that these are mere coats of tranquility varnished over the wound excels it.

The great eccentric Ryūtarō Kitahara came back from the Second World War to tell Hisamatsu: "Sitting is all I have." Hisamatsu shot back: "Sitting won't do!" Out of the resolution to that contradiction came what I quoted at the outset of Part Two—Kitahara's final sentence to an introductory lesson on how to practice the meditation that was the core of his life: "Try various ways of meditating, but when you are forced to confront what to do when all of them have failed—that is the essence of meditation." The limits of the glory of meditation—that its splendor rarely irreversibly shatters disquiet as the default mode of consciousness—resuscitate the question: beautified prison or prison break?

11. MEDITATION AS AN AFFIRMATION OF LIFE WITHIN THE IMPRISONING CONDITIONS

Meditation as the Struggle against Negation

Call the problem of the self I have described in this book *the negating force*. It is the force that pulverizes the heart. It may take the form of anxiety. It may take the form of dissatisfaction with all possible things, or of emptiness. It may take the form of loneliness, or of an acute consciousness of the burdensome character of life, or of the threat of an unfulfilled or meaningless existence. One may experience it as the sense of sin that requires no action to *be* sin. As the agony of squandering one's existence, and not simply through the waste of time, but through the realization that were one to plan systematically and wisely every second of one's life, one still could not shake the feeling in some deep and troubling sense of life being squandered. One may experience the force as the dread of death that attacks, even in the absence of immediate or specific threat, or whenever one fears that one's final thought will be: "You cannot—*must* not—live as you have lived." The dominating form may vary from person to person, or within the life of a person. One form or another, no one escapes negation.[60] The conscripts in the spiritual quest are those in whom this negation explodes into one's life in such a way as to subordinate every other concern. Tillich therefore called it the "ultimate concern," the concern with what concerns us ultimately. Hisamatsu called it, more darkly, the ultimate negation.

This force of the negation, once known, leaves us but three possibilities: (1) To affirm existence, as Tillich would say, "in spite of" or in the face of, the negating conditions without being able to remove them. (2) To be liberated from, by dissolving, the negating force. (3) To succumb to the negation through the failure to achieve a sufficiently meaningful life affirmation; the failure, that is, to achieve (1) or (2).

The fourth possibility—to deny the existence of the negation—is no longer available to anyone on the spiritual quest, conscript or volunteer.

Meditative Existentialism: Self-Affirmation without Liberation

For a year, in Japan, I went through hell over what may seem from the outside as the trivial decision to switch from the half lotus to the full lotus position in meditation. It was a period when I lived only a few blocks away from the Zen Buddhist philosopher Masao Abe and was frequently at his home. One night I challenged him—in agony and confusion—whether the pain was worth it. During that year I had befriended a young Japanese man, Toyoshima-san, who shocked me by the life-staking ferociousness with which he meditated. Abe had known him for years. He said, in response: "Do you think Toyoshima-san has the luxury to ask the question you just put to me?" Then, as I was walking out the door, Abe added, "Very few people have the spiritual courage of Toyoshima-san."

This unassuming schoolteacher, who cannot bear to hurt anyone, said to me once: "I no longer sit to break through. I sit because I cannot stop." At sixty-three, after forty years possessed of a courage in meditation that strikes fear into many of those that know him, Toyoshima-san is fully aware that he may die in the same predicament as when he began.

Though nothing could have been further from his intention, it was Toyoshima-san who enforced upon me the prospect that my own meditation might turn out to be, at best, a weapon in the battle against negation, rather than a means to liberation. In Paul Tillich's *The Courage to Be,* courage is described as the capacity to affirm oneself in spite of the forces that negate us, whether those forces negate from outside (the threats posed by others, by nature) or within (loneliness, anxiety, despondency, fear). The greater one's power of self-affirmation "in spite of" the negating threats, the greater one's existence. Jesus, nailed to a cross and praying, "Father, forgive them, for they know not what they do," is a symbol, even for me as an atheist, of ultimate affirmation in the face of the negation of hatred, loneliness, and death. In *Love, Power, and Justice,* Tillich writes:

> Every being resists the negation against itself. The self-affirmation of a being is correlate to the power of being it embodies. It is greater in man than in animals and in some men greater than others. A life process is the more powerful, the more non-being it can include in its self-affirmation, without being destroyed by it. The neurotic can include only a little non-being, the average man a limited amount, the creative man a large amount, God—symbolically speaking—an infinite amount. The

self-affirmation of a being in spite of non-being is the expression of its power of being . . . Power is the possibility of self-affirmation in spite of internal and external negation.[61]

Proponents of eastern religious philosophies often deride existentialism as futile or inferior for not having the power to dispel the anxiety, the loneliness, the threats to meaning it delineates. But the hard truth is that most practitioners of these religions have likewise failed to dispel them. Awakening, Oneness, Nonduality, etc., may well be the ultimate ideal, but an unachieved ideal leaves one with the problematic real. All the unawakened meditators I know either explicitly or implicitly bring to bear one of two existentialist categories: courage or bad faith. Either they press on despite the persistence of the "I" that negates them in the earnest hope of one day being free of it, or they declare their meditation transformative prematurely, writing checks for more money than they have in the bank.

Meditative Existentialism: The Counterforce

What I call for myself "the counterforce" is the fundamental element by which my life is sustained. Induced in meditation, it can be injected into pain, whether of the body or of the mind. The counterforce may be initially as tiny as a centimeter within the field of physical or emotional distress but, once present, this point of composed pleasure and vitality, however surrounded by pain, can be brought to bear against it. By continued effort, finally effortlessly, the pleasure deepens and widens. The force of the pleasure, its energized stillness, seeps into, and begins to counter, the negating force of the pain. The stillness and turmoil, pleasure and pain, may be experienced simultaneously. The pleasure, originating in the center of the mind and spreading outward, or in the periphery of the mind and seeping in, or generated at some specific point and gradually suffusing body and mind, expands and strengthens. At times—not always—it begins to get the upper hand. Then the pain may be banished; I can move from affliction or torpor to extreme well-being in the course of an hour. The well-being may last for hours, or days. At its best it can thwart the force of illness, loneliness, and heartbreak; the depth, power, degree, and duration of this capacity have no predetermined limit apart from the limit subject to all duration—transience. At its least, it gives an inch of sanctuary, albeit sanctuary under siege. That inch can be sufficient, amidst grave difficulty, to affirm a life.

Of the ways of redecorating the prison, meditation offers one of the great interior designs. It is of the sabbath, in the Jewish sense that the day of rest be the foretaste of paradise. DeMartino once said that any serious meditator would have hundreds of what psychologist Abraham Maslow called "peak experiences."

Anyone who cultivates meditation assiduously will know its consolation, its vast sense of relief. It makes life without hope hard to conceive. It offers periods of freedom that few know. But it is the freedom of the Taoist sage Lieh Tzu. He was so free, we are told, that he could ride the wind, but his freedom, chides Chuang Tzu, needed the wind, hence he was not free.

For the negating power, uncrushed, reasserts itself, however many of the manifest forms of negation are checked or quelled by periods of ecstatic transcendence. It will bring to an end the tranquility gained by merging with the wound, no less than the tranquility gained through techniques of meditation. Disquiet inevitably resurges from the depths of consciousness, sometimes concurrent with the joy. Succeed in all else but leave this pain unresolved and life fails—this is its mantra. The Zen master Ta Hui (1089–1163) describes it as a red-hot iron ball one can neither digest nor spit out. The seventeenth-century Japanese samurai turned Zen monk Suzuki Shōsan called it the "great matter" that assailed him every morning from loins to chest between 3 and 5 AM. I used to think they spoke metaphorically. I know better now.

12. THE SIMULTANEITY OF STALEMATE AND CHECK

Lash yourself to the mast of consciousness; the joy that comes— standing, walking, sitting, or lying—does not dissolve the wound.

Richard DeMartino argued endlessly that meditative ecstasy (*samadhi*) is but a temporary transcendence of the problematic structure of the unawakened self. Hisamatsu's fundamental koan in one of its forms: "When meditation will not do, what do you do?"

So the path of meditation is also cut, but it is not really cut. It is endlessly available, like so many other paths that will not do, and this is the dilemma. The self-as-problem must be check-mated. Instead it is stalemated.

The "I" is stuck precisely because of its inability to get truly stuck. Self-consciousness is possessed of a fluidity that dooms subjectivity to slip out of every endeavor to arrest itself, much like a person unable to drive the final nail into his coffin except from a vantage point external to the coffin. Stuck because it is unstuck, if the "I" could become stuck it would truly become unstuck. For again, to be irreversibly stuck, cornered, dead-locked is the necessary prelude to the liberation which, according to Hisamatsu, emerges with the dissolution of the ultimate impasse. "When cornered there is a change; where there is a change, there is a passing through."

Seen from another angle, while whatever the "I" does *will not do*, the "I" cannot but continue to be and to do. The translation "will not do" in Hisamatsu's fundamental koan is a rendering of the Japanese *ikenai,* which means "of no avail," "of no use," "wrong," or "hopeless," but literally can be translated as "cannot go," "does not go," or "won't go." One way of looking at the dilemma is that everything that one undertakes in an effort to solve the problem "does not go" precisely because the "I" cannot stop going. The only way in which this going can be stopped is for "all routes to be extinguished." But human awareness, by its very nature involved in an inevitable or "infinite" regress, makes this impossible. This regress means simply that human consciousness can always take an additional step back: I not only know that I am I and that the world is the world; I know that I know, and know that I know that I know. This feature of self-consciousness not only enables (as an aspect of human freedom) but forces (as an aspect of human destiny) the "I" to be thrust out of both itself and its world. Hence Tillich's remark that every human being has a world "set over against himself, from which he is separated and to which he belongs at the same time," and Rousseau's belief that we know life only from its margins. It is this feature that gives us the awareness of space and time. This feature that gives us the capacity to project onto our future a way forward. Not only can we do so, we cannot but do so. The continual emergence of a new "route" is unavoidable. So long as we are able to step back and observe ourselves, we are powerless to prevent the casting of a way before us that we then have the possibility to "traverse." Thus Hisamatsu's previously quoted observation that "there is always some kind of a way out" which the "I" has *already taken* even at the moment of resolving to bar all avenues shut. Thus U. G. Krishnamurti's koan: "The aspiration [for a solution] is part of your consciousness. That has to come to an end. There is nothing you can do to stop it. In other words, you cannot but do sadhana [spiritual practice]; you are doomed that way. Even if you drop sadhana, it creates a struggle in you. You will replace it with another kind of sadhana."[62]

The reality that whatever it does will not do places the "I" in perennial check. Still, though checked, it is never mated. The "I" retains its ability to engage in another move, and has no means to rid itself of this mobility even should it desire to do so. The functioning of self-consciousness therefore involves the "I" in a *stalemate* from which it can in no way be extricated. Unable to free itself from the check that blocks every attempt to resolve its dilemma, it is similarly unable to establish the checkmate that would be the ultimate impasse of these endeavors. The unceasing regress of subjectivity means that the "I" eludes every check, only to be faced with another check that it cannot but elude. Check cannot be circumvented; checkmate cannot be precipitated.

This chess analogy has its limit. For there can be no time lapse between the eluding of one check and the onset of another.

The "I" is in check and out of it simultaneously, never sufficiently in check to be mated, never out of check to the extent
of not also being already checked. The Alexandrian poet C. P.
Cavafy's line, "Where every step now tightens the noose," in his
poem "The City,"[63] is true precisely in that each step is a slack-
ening of the noose as well. An integral element of the nature of
the perennial check is the inevitable eluding of it.

13. SHATTERING THE IMPASSE

I once said to DeMartino: "Hisamatsu says 'all routes must be
cut.' The 'I' can't do that." DeMartino said: "Now you're in
the dilemma." In Kyoto, Masao Abe had said: "Corner yourself
as much as possible." Many nights I am caught in what I call
"duplex" or "second story" meditation. Pleasure in the upper
floors, in the basement the iron ball that can neither be digested
nor vomited out.

It's the basement that counts, ultimately. You try to crush
that ball, it will not yield; or in meditative intoxication for a
while it disappears. You try to enter it; sooner or later you are
thrust again outside. Often, at the first touch of the mind to its
own wound, I retch. After that it moves toward effortlessness.

I once asked DeMartino: "Should you try to break through
or should you try to let go?" He said: "If your breaking through
is different from your letting go there's something wrong." You

try to break through. You try to let go. You can do neither. Later I asked: "Should you try to break through or let it carry you across?" "Let it carry you across," he answered. "Like a mantra?" I asked. "No, not like a mantra." A year after, I reminded him of that conversation. He shook his head, saying: "I shouldn't have said 'Let it carry you across' either." Once he said: "To break through you must be totally active, totally passive. I, yet not I." Toyoshima-san, the meditation Prometheus, used to say when I asked about his superhuman sitting: "I've already given up." This confused me, since his meditation was relentless. Until, when seven years later I got back to Japan from America, he added: "But you can't really give up, either. When all effort won't do, and giving up won't do, what do you do?"

I remember watching the television show *Ramar of the Jungle* as a child. In it Ramar, approaching a hidden tribe in the forest, would suddenly be encircled by a prison cell of thrown spears. So these conversations, some from decades ago, strike in eternal ambush in my darkened apartment or while I'm brushing my teeth, blocking advance or retreat at the toe and the heel.

Kafka tells the parable of the running mouse that fears falling over the edge of the abyss, only to find the equal fear of walls suddenly appearing and steadily closing in on him as he is forced toward the trap. The cat says the way out of his fix is simple: "Just change direction!" So the mouse does and the cat gobbles him up. I long thought of it as a tale of structural entrapment; now I see it as liberation. It is the path I follow, the one path left. Change direction and be swallowed by the cat, which is consciousness.

Suzuki Shōsan, who each morning inscribed the ideogram for death twenty times on his chest with his finger, relates how "the great matter" rose from loins to breast in the hours before each dawn. I know that rising like a brother, like a feared step-father. I long fled it, even through meditation. I yield to it now. It is the wound of consciousness—causeless anxiety—surging through the body in what I think of as its "liquefied" form. Cease resisting it and liquid anxiety eventually begins to crystal-lize. This is the crucial sentence and I hope I'm up to its explica-tion. For it is the final congealing of liquid anxiety, liquid lone-liness, into "crystal" that is required, in what Zen refers to as the "great doubt block" (*daigidan*) or "mass of doubt," the su-preme deadlock that Hisamatsu calls the "causal foundation"—or precondition—of awakening.

DeMartino once said the greatest sentence he ever wrote was: "It is not that the ego *has* a problem. The ego *is* the prob-lem." Yet however intolerable, so long as the problem of the "I" stands in dualistic relation to the "I" who tries to resolve it—even if the "I" knows this problem as that which it in fact *is*—the problem remains a problem that the "I" *has*. This duality, between problem and the one who has it, entails the very cleavage of subject and object that must be extirpated for the "I" to be blocked from further regress or progress so that "all routes are cut" and checkmate achieved. The "I" is unable to precipitate this deadlock through its own efforts. Yet in its failed efforts, the tension between the imperative for and impossibility of a solution gains in intensity, eating away at the "I" until it is utterly incapable of dislocating itself from its problem and thereby transforming it into an object of contemplation. Herein, the "I," like Jonah swallowed by the whale, may be so thoroughly ensnared or grasped by its problem that it can be said, metaphorically speaking, to be "in" the dilemma. But such a condition is likewise insufficient. Whether seeking to attack the problem from outside or from in, the duality between problem and bearer of the problem persists. To grasp or grapple with the problem will not do. But to be grasped by or ensnared in the problem likewise will not do. Only when the "I" is not simply *in* the dilemma, but fully actualized *as* the dilemma, can the ultimate deadlock or great doubt be said to have been actualized. What must happen, says DeMartino, speaking in Zen terms:

> is for the ego,[64] physically as well as mentally, to come
> to be this radical contradiction or "great doubt block."
> The "great doubt" (or "great doubt block") is noth-
> ing other than the intrinsic predicament of the ego in

ego-consciousness thoroughly and climactically exacerbated. The penultimate purpose of the koan—as well as of the accompanying methodology of zazen [seated meditation], sesshin [intensive meditation retreat], and *sanzen* [interview with a Zen teacher]—is, consequently, to get the ego to arouse, to accentuate, to bring entirely to the fore, and then (rather than as a regressing subject to bear the burden of) to crystallize locked-in-itself-non-regressively the dualistic contradiction that, as ego, it veritably is.[65]

Solely when the "I," no longer enduring or in any way *beset by* its predicament, has become "locked-in-itself-non-regressively" *as* the predicament does further regress or progress become impossible. Since the problem is thoroughly "I," consciousness is no longer capable of dislodging itself from the problem even to the slightest extent. The ability to regress definitively curtailed, there can be no distancing oneself from the problem, hence no possibility of encountering the problem in any external or objectified form. All routes of body and mind, and even the very being of the "I," congeal into one great impasse. Hisamatsu says of this impasse: "In terms of the intellect it is absolute contradiction, in terms of the emotions, absolute anguish, in terms of the will, absolute dilemma." It is the supreme and simultaneous deadlock of human thinking, feeling, and doing. He describes it as the absolute cornering in which

STEVE ANTINOFF

one can neither advance, retreat, nor stand still; when one no longer *faces*, as in existentialism, but *becomes* the "wall of ultimate negation."

The Chinese Zen classic *The Gateless Barrier* demands, if the barrier is to be penetrated, the "producing of a doubt which penetrates the entire self, pervading all 360 joints and 84,000 pores." Too long I took this as a metaphor: a mistake on my part. The surge of inherent disquiet, as it pulls one in, inflates body and mind like a balloon. I call that surge, for myself, the glacier. Lashed to it, I ride out my nights. The glacier, the agitated tensing of consciousness, creeps toward coagulation if ridden without pause. This occurs refractory to one's control. Just as the "I" is the recipient, against its will in one sense, of its own consciousness, and of the wound that mars consciousness, so one is the passive recipient of the surge as well. As water turns to ice, the mind, too, literally starts to freeze. This ice-cold clarity is the greatest delight I know. Hakuin's autobiographical description immediately before his awakening is the culmination of the glacier's surge: "Suddenly a great doubt manifested itself before me. It was as though I were frozen solid in the midst of a sheet of ice extending tens of thousands of miles. A purity filled my breast and I could neither go forward nor retreat." But without that total crystallization the "glacier" is a thrilling, life-enriching pleasure that resolves nothing. Only semi-congealed, which is as

far as I have been able to take it, the wound inevitably hemor-
rhages into the pleasure.

No doubt this accounts for a portion of psychological and
psychosomatic illness. The wound, the natural koan, if aroused
from its latency but not crystallized (because not "brought
entirely to the fore"), comes at a price. I was long puzzled by
Hakuin's assertion that what is called "Zen sickness," which
felled him for three years, was caused by bad motivation, since
his own motivation was unrelenting. I think what he means is
that it is hazardous for the wound to impose itself on consciousness and fester uncongealed or half congealed where it cannot
resolve. Then one is left between two stools, unable to annul
awareness of the wound or to transcend it. Thomas Mann writes
in *Death in Venice* of those in whom talent presents the physical
frame with a destiny it cannot bear up to. In origin and symptom, the risks of the spiritual quest and the artistic quest are not
dissimilar. Freud wrote toward the end of his life: "The individual dies of his internal conflicts." DeMartino, when asked why
those in Auschwitz did not get enlightened, answered: "Despair
is not enough. The despair must be focused." By this he means
the despair must be crystallized, brought to the impasse that is
not an object but oneself.

Ramana Maharshi says: "The doubt must be uprooted. The
doubter must be uprooted." So much chatter these days about

the need to "let go," all of it missing that the letting go of objects, physical or mental, is endless and solves nothing at the root—it is the subject that must be let go. Try to get into the root; you can't. Yet you must. Try again . . . and again—the root of the wound, of self, of consciousness, the wound that is never an object, recedes. Actively plunge into the source, or passively sink into it in a way that is not temporary; you can't. Yet you must. The strengthening tension between "must" and "can't" pulls in opposing directions as on a taut rubber band. The "must" drives you to further effort despite the "can't." The "can't" exposes the inadequacy of effort despite the "must." Crucified on the bisection of "can't" and "must," "impossibility" and "necessity," "will not do" and "what do you do?," the mind in search of the source of its wound drops downward. The receding wound drops downward further still. In Zen they talk of placing the koan in the lower abdomen. DeMartino said the monks in Japan told him to "get it down in the balls." Later he told me: "You can't stop there, either. Get it down into the center of the universe."

Endless bouts, between the counterforce of brightness-pleasure-calm-energy and the hemorrhage, the negating vise of the wound. The mental icy beauty of the Snow Queen's domicile flooded by horror, flooded by beauty; two sides, as in the Japanese idiom, of the same sheet of paper. The prison break requires something else: *the tension between the impossibility of and necessity for a solution brought to the ultimate pitch.* Hisamatsu calls it "ultimate crisis"—the struggle within consciousness between "can't" and "must" reaching the "point of no return" that strips away any certainty one will survive.

This is the bodhi tree, invisible and placeless, beyond the vow or decision: either enlightenment or death. U. G. Krishnamurti describes *his* experience of his ultimate crisis, right before his enlightenment, stretched out on his wife's bed certain he was dying (she told him he was full of it and left the room):

> The whole life energy was moving to some focal point. Where it was, I don't know. Then a point arrived where the whole thing looked as if the aperture of a camera was trying to close itself. (It is the only simile I can think of. The way I am describing this is quite different from the way things happened at the time, because there was nobody there thinking in such terms . . .) So the aperture was trying to close itself, and something there was trying to keep it open. Then after a while there was no will to do anything, not even to prevent the aperture from closing itself. Suddenly, as it were, it closed. I don't know what happened after that.[66]

I know this aperture, the closing shutter of consciousness. But always as an object, something I'm pulled into; therefore something to be thrust out of later with the problem still unresolved. Yet the aperture is not an object. It is the source of consciousness stripped of every object, without foothold. At the extreme limit of the contradiction of being an "I" the aperture fights simultaneously to stay open and to give way.

Hisamatsu describes his own realization of it—and its shattering—on December 3, 1915:

It was in addition the *rohatsu sesshin* [meditation retreat], the most demanding of the year. It involved, both physically and mentally, anguish of a kind the author had never before experienced. The extreme, murderous tension of the meditation hall, which is encountered nowhere else, the absolutely relentless urgings of the head monk and the cold December wind which blew into the hall through the open windows—these drove the author to the limits of fear and shuddering. Because he was not accustomed to sitting *zazen*, the pain of the full lotus position and the stiffness in his neck, back, and hips grew worse with every session of meditation. The author was at the point where he could just barely maintain the seated posture, grimacing and gritting his teeth. He was on the verge of having his efforts to solve the *koan* stolen away by the pain. And yet, at the same time, his private meetings with the rōshi, both voluntary and compulsory (*dokusan* and *sōsan*) pressed in moment by moment, driving him on, regardless of his feelings, to further efforts in his grappling with the *koan*. Body and mind, he proceeded on into ever greater extremity. Whenever the rōshi entered the room, he became an impregnable mountain fortress, progressively cutting off the possibility of climbing out of the chasm of one's predicament. His single eye, pure white, glared with a killer's intensity.

By the third day, the author had himself become a "great doubt block," black, and with no means of escape left open in the entirety of his existence, not even one the size of the hole in a needle. He had been thrown into, literally, the realm of inescapable and absolute death. In this state, it was not that the author had taken a particular problem, of whatever kind, as an object of his concentration, as a matter which must be unraveled, and then come to a dead end, unable to approach the problem from any other direction whatsoever; not that he had taken up a universal, all-encompassing problem as the object to be solved, and then, unable to solve it, become attached to this problem in the depths of himself, where it remained a pressing doubt. It was rather that the author himself became, in a total and unified expression of his existence, a "great doubt block." In the *Mumonkan [The Gateless Barrier]*, this kind of experience is described as the "producing of a doubt which penetrates the entire self, pervading all 360 joints and 84,000 pores." As is often said in Zen, it is as though a rat were to crawl into a bamboo tube and become stuck there, as though one were to climb to the tip of a pole 300 feet tall, and then find oneself unable to advance, to descend again, or to maintain one's

position. In this *cul-de-sac*, the author was visited by
an unexpected moment in which, just as the expression
"Cornered there is a change, where there is a change,
there is a break through" would have it, the great doubt
block that he had become collapsed, shattered from
within. And even the rugged mountain fortress, which
had been his perception of the rōshi until this point,
caved in simultaneously, leaving not a trace behind it.
There no longer remained the space to insert a hair between the rōshi and the author. At this moment, the
author gained for the first time positive confirmation
of his true self, formless and self-residing, and simultaneously was able for the first time to truly converse
with the authentic being of the rōshi. He truly came to
know that the words of Master Mumon—"Grasping
hands with the patriarchs of history, and going along
together with them, I have joined eyebrows with the
patriarchs in seeing as they see, joined ears in hearing as
they hear"—were no deception. As is maintained by the
expression, "One cutting cuts all things; one attainment
is to attain all things," all the problems that the author
had been unable to resolve for so many years were at
this moment fundamentally resolved, at their very root.
The author attained to a realm of incomparable joy,
which he had never before entered into. At this point in
the *rohatsu sesshin*, the author gained eternal life, and
was able to consummately realize absolute existence
and absolute value.[67]

13 RESOLVING IT

ETERNAL LIFE · ABSOLUTE EXISTENCE · ABSOLUTE VALUE

The poem Hisamatsu composed on his seventy-seventh birthday begins: "Having lived zero years seventy-seven times." And, in an interview two years before his death he wrote: "With my birthday this year I turned eighty-eight. When I was young I was weak physically, but I've managed to live a surprisingly long life. And yet, I don't believe that my age now is my true age. 'True Age' is something apart from one's physical age. I was convinced of that when I broke through my first koan. It's the same thing as saying that there is no 'age.' In other words, that there is no 'life-and-death.'"

In one of his five death poems he wrote:

Who would say I am now dying
Not knowing me originally of no birth

In another:

Dying without death, born without birth
I sport through the triple world.

At eighty-eight he said:

Even before I attained *kenshō* [awakening; literally, seeing one's (true) nature], I had an intellectual understanding of the words of Kanzan Egen [1277–1360], the founder of Myōshinji Monastery—"For Egen's true self there is no life-and-death"—but it was not until the time when I broke through my first *koan* that I concretely and experientially came to know that I truly was not subject to life-and-death. At that time I thought: "Egen has said something really profound. He has really spoken the truth." I still think so. And thus it is that I consider that I do not die. There is truly in this world that which does not die. The problem is only that people are not awakened to this truth. Without clarifying the problem of life-and-death there can be no awakening to one's true nature.[68]

"Clarifying the problem of life-and-death" means overturning the primary fact of ordinary human consciousness—the awareness of being an "I" that is moving, in Heidegger's phrase, "towards death." Consciousness of one's finitude without the simultaneous consciousness of one's infinitude is false consciousness. "Kanzan's remark: 'In me there is no life-and-death,'" says Hisamatsu, "is not strange at all. One comes to clearly realize that, on the contrary, it is saying that there *is* life-and-death which is mistaken."[69]

Being without life-and-death, without time, has, for Hisamatsu, nothing to do with an afterlife, transmigration of an ongoing soul, reincarnation, or God:

> Being without life-and-death never means that there is no life and death in the ordinary sense. It is not that one lives forever, or that not dying in the ordinary sense, one lives temporally a long life. "Being without life-and-death" means that there is no birth, and because there is no birth, there is also no death. This is the true eternal life.[70]

Eternal life grasped *now*, by slaying time, as everyday life: "While living and dying one does not live and die, while not living and dying one lives and dies"[71] writes Hisamatsu. And, "The Self of no life-death nature goes on in the midst of life-and-death, forming history while transcending it."[72] Hisamatsu likens the liberated self to a spider who spins its web without ever being caught in it. "Such a life of unobstructed freedom . . . is extricated from every fetter. In the midst of life-and-death it cannot be injured by life or death; rid of life-and-death it plays within it; . . . though in time and space it is restricted by neither."[73] He calls this "the consummate unfetteredness . . . of the 'Samadhi of absolutely untrammeled play'"[74] through which one shatters the tragedy of finitude, "play[ing] freely amid the thick woods of what formerly constituted self-agonizing illusions,"[75] "enter[ing] the garden of life-and-death, freely taking on the forms of life and death yet neither living nor dying."[76]

Richard DeMartino labeled this the true Divine Comedy. Socrates displayed it, turning his trial and death into a farce. Whitman had it from the first stanza of himself—a loafer at his ease for whom a single blade of grass is all that is needed. Chuang Tzu had it from cover to cover, author of the greatest book of spiritual comedy ever written, the unintended foil to a Jesus whose teeth have never once been seen in the history of art. Ryūtarō Kitahara had it, thrust into crisis first by watching his father, Hakushū Kitahara, the greatest Japanese poet of his era, die in agony, later brought to the breaking point during the war by carrying out orders to bayonet a Chinese captive who had been bound to a tree, then emerging, after years of struggle with Hisamatsu, as a dead-serious comic whose antics subverted the alleged necessity of severity in the meditation hall. Then there's the eighth-century monk Teng Yin-feng:

> [who] when he was about to die, asked: "I have seen
> monks die sitting and lying, but have any died stand-
> ing?" "Yes, some," was the reply. "How about upside
> down?" "Never have we seen such a thing!" Whereupon
> Teng stood on his head and died. When it was time to

carry him to the funeral pyre he remained upside down [rigor mortis having set in], to the wonder of those who came to view the remains, and the consternation of those who would dispose of them. Finally his younger sister, a nun, came and grumbling at him said, "When you were alive you took no notice of laws and customs, and even now that you are dead you are making a nuisance of yourself!" And with that she poked him with her finger, felling him with a thud; and the procession carried him away to the crematorium. In this way Teng, assuming what, from the remarks of his sister, was not the unfamiliar role of the clown, expressed his achievement of spiritual freedom, his liberation from a desperate clinging to life and anxiety over self, and therefore his transcendence of the problem of death.[77]

This cosmic loafing (Hisamatsu calls it the Calm Self in the midst of the most strenuous activity[78]), and the *samadhi*—or the achievement of Oneness—that engenders it, can only be free if eternal. Hisamatsu writes:

It is said that Plotinus experienced the ecstasy of "One" four times in his life. But if the One is merely this sort of thing, it is momentary and passing, an experience of only one time and one place. This experience does not constitute eternal subjectivity, for the true One is never just one particular experience. The falling away of mind and body is eternal, never something from which one can separate. That which never separates is the Self, the True Self. The True Self is the eternal Self, a Self unrestricted by time and space. Accordingly, it is the unborn-undying Self, the Self without life-and-death, the Self existing as Nirvana. Therefore, this is never something one becomes and then separates from. As indicated in the expression "Ordinary Mind is the Way," the True Self is the ordinary, constant mind, which never changes or is parted from. The condition in zazen wherein a person experiences a good feeling that disappears at the end of sitting is a mere illusion. True zazen must be unborn-undying zazen functioning in the midst of life-and-death . . . Whether standing, sitting, lying, thinking, living or dying, this always is the Self. Only this kind of Self can be designated as the True Self. A self differing from this cannot even be called a "self."[79]

In other words, meditative *samadhi* that is restricted by time brings the inevitable return to disquiet—the default mode of human life. Nor will meditation do if it is spatially restricted to the position of sitting, or restricted by a breakable concentration. Hisamatsu writes:

Sitting is something eternal; in other words it is the [awakened] Subject. It is this Subject which stands. Standing does not mean rising from out of [some particular] condition of sitting. It is the "sitting" which stands.[80]

Ryūtarō Kitahara records Hisamatsu pressing him: "What is the sitting that is not sitting in the full lotus but continues whether one is walking, standing, sitting or lying?" Hisamatsu rejects the common admonition that one rise composed from the meditation hall so as to maintain what has been gained in the sitting posture and integrate it into one's daily life, insisting that even if one trips over his feet and stumbles out the hall, meditation as the eternal awakened Subject—or "I"—cannot be lost. He has no interest in temporary transcendences or partial solutions. "What I want to speak of . . . is not a fragmentary, anticipatory overcoming, but a fundamental resolution that goes down to the root."[81] "The solution of branch problems alone will not bring about the solution of the root problem."[82] He continues: "So long as the root-source, ultimate suffering, is not broken through, we will be eternally unable to be freed from our suffering."[83] If the root is not extirpated "it is a matter of course that the sprouts will again shoot forth."[84]

In his autobiography Hisamatsu describes his own awakening in just such radical terms.

As is maintained by the expression, "One cutting cuts all things; one attainment is to attain all things," all the problems that the author had been unable to resolve for so many years were at this moment [of awakening] fundamentally resolved at their very root.[85]

The "I" Hisamatsu attained is attested to in various religions but depends on none of them. No single religion owns it. Yet religions in the plural do not own it either. The Hindus call it Self. The Buddhists call it no-self. But that is a scholar's difference. One of the great T'ang dynasty Buddhists, Shi T'ou, cried out at the moment of his awakening: "There is no self. There is nothing that is not the Self."

What counts, independent of the cultural colorings given it by the various mystics and religions, is the bare realization of the not-twoness of "I" and "not-I." Hisamatsu names it "Myself [which] goes beyond internal and external."[86]

> This *I* differs from the ordinary "I" that stands in opposition to other selves; this is the *I* that has eliminated the ordinary "I." This *I* no longer simply distinguishes itself from other selves.[87]

From the perspective of that "I," each encountered phenomenon is simultaneously transitory and unborn-undying, is at once itself, not itself, and so every other. Its totality (its absolute existence) is its absolute value. Siddhartha, picking up a stone in the closing pages of Hesse's novel, says:

> [T]his is a stone, it is also an animal, it is also a god, it is also Buddha. I do not revere it and love it because it may some day become one thing or another, but because it has long been everything—and it is precisely the fact of

being a stone, of its appearing to me as a stone now and today that makes me love it, and see value and meaning in each of its cavities . . . each [stone] is *Brahman*; but at the same time and just as much, it is a stone.[88]

The not twoness of "I" and "not-I" in turn has its basis in the not-twoness of "I am" and "I am not." *Since I am not*, I am without time, without beginning and end, without life and death. *Since I am*, I am time-bound, death-bound, subject to decay. Chuang Tzu calls it "hiding the universe in the universe," which means to hide the universe in the self by hiding the self in its not. Hakuin proclaims it in his adopted name: "Hidden in the White." Richard DeMartino expresses it in his restatement of Gertrude Stein: "Rose is not a rose is the whole universe is a rose." The thirteenth-century Andalusian Muslim mystic and poet Shustari writes:

After extinction I came out, and I
Eternal now am, though not as I.
Yet who am I, O I, but I?[89]

Whitman declares he is not contained within his hat and boots, to look for him under our boot soles. But what is not contained within one's hat and boots is not exhausted *in things* either.

Stephen Jourdain, ex–real estate agent, owner of a bed-and-breakfast in Corsica, in his book *Radical Awakening* describes his awakening at sixteen—when he penetrated the "I" of Descartes's *I think therefore I am*—with the simple phrase: "I am without being." The editor of this book, Gilles Farcet, confirms that this "definitive and 'crucial experience' of which he [Jourdain] declared himself to be the victim of at the age of sixteen, had no connection to any religious or esoteric tradition whatsoever." Jourdain himself insists: "You know, I don't believe in God, being a rationalist and an atheist." When speaking of his "I" he sounds exactly like Hisamatsu: "The astonishing thing is that this pure subject is infinite consciousness, infinite existence, and infinite value." On the reading of books about awakening, Jourdain says: "It then suffices for me to examine the texts that one sets before my eyes. If I find 'I am,' without 'I am not this,' it's not worth the trouble to continue. We're not talking about the same thing." He writes, "Before the awakening I experienced all sorts of extraordinary states—infinite consciousness of myself, etc., etc. I could have very well already considered myself awakened. When I describe these experiences, I sometimes wonder where the difference lies. Yet, it exists precisely in the fact that prior to the awakening the saber didn't thrust forth. One feels [in the partial experiences] the 'I am' without simultaneously feeling the 'I am not.'" And, "If I precisely describe my experience, I find it in the destructive aspect of Zen—the 'I am not' aspect—at the same time as the surging forth of the individual 'I am.'"[90]

The expressions "unborn-undying," "without life and death," and "'I' as 'not-I'" may be clearer in the light of Chuang Tzu's: ". . . after he had done away with past and present he was able to enter where there is no life and death. That which kills life does not die; that which gives life to life does not live."[91] What Chuang Tzu calls "that" Hisamatsu calls "Formless Self." One awakens to one's Self as the eternal moving finger in Omar Khayyam's *Rubaiyat*: "The moving finger writes, and having writ, moves on."[92] The protagonist of *The Atheists' Monastery*, colliding with this unmoved-mover in the person of the monastery master in the act of snatching a firefly, says it's:

> as if you were listening to Mozart's wind sextet in a concert hall. You hear in the succession of notes the oboe, the clarinet and the horn. Each sound of each instrument appears, then disappears, as each new cluster of notes carries forward the flux of music. Then comes the adagio. Suddenly you are arrested not simply by the sound, but what you have never before noticed and could not possibly have expected to notice: the air that is the source common to each sound, the air that is the life-source and life-force of every sound that is ever made by any instrument that lives by the breath of man. Each sound formed by the oboe, by the clarinet, dissolves; the air cannot dissolve. It can only produce sound out of itself and absorb sound into itself; sound

that is nothing but itself. The sounds it forms itself into are born and die; this creating-dissolving power that gives life to sound and to all things and takes their life away—unaffected by what it creates, untouched by what it destroys—is older than birth and cannot die.

So Hisamatsu proclaims: "Unborn, undying. This is the answer to my fundamental koan: 'When whatever you do will not do, what do you do?'"[93] In the same vein he frequently quotes Shidō Bunan's poem:

> *While alive be a dead man*
> *thoroughly dead*
> *then, do as you will*
> *all will be well*[94]

Having killed life and death in the midst of life and death (the meaning of "while alive be dead")—*whatever you do will do*. But this answer must precede doing (just as the problem preceded doing). As Hisamatsu puts it: "the answer must be out even before the question is asked."[95] Only in this way is the koan he gave to Ryūtarō Kitahara—"Drink the tea without using your mouth!"—resolved in a favorite story of Hisamatsu:

> In the tenth-century China there lived a Zen master named Dasui Fazhen [Ta-sui Fa-chên]. When asked: "When life-and-death has come what do you do?" he

answered promptly. "When served tea, I take tea, when served a meal I take a meal. I am afraid some people might take this to be beside the point. But, on the contrary, this hits the bull's eye.[96]

The koan "When life-and-death has come what do you do?" has its exact parallel in the koan put to the Chinese Zen master Yunmen (864–949) by a monk: "When life and death have come, how do you get rid of it?" Yunmen's answer— "Where is it?"—is his way of affirming that there is no life or death. What Hisamatsu insisted above for meditation, "true zazen must be unborn-undying zazen functioning in the midst of life-and-death," holds true for drinking or anything else: it must be unborn-undying drinking in the midst of life-and-death, the drinking of that which kills and gives life but is neither born nor dies. Hisamatsu's contemporary, the Zen master Zenkei Shibayama, sheds light on this point in his own commentary on Nan-ch'üan's remark "Ordinary Mind is the Tao [or Way]":

> The ordinary mind Zen upholds is not our dualistic ordinary mind, but it has to be the ordinary mind attained by satori [awakening]. Master Keizan, of Sōtō Zen in Japan, was suddenly enlightened when he listened to his teacher Master Tettsu's teishō [or Zen talk] on "Ordinary Mind is Tao." Keizan declared, "I have got it!" to which his teacher retorted, "How have

you got it?" "A jet-black iron ball speeds through the dark night!" This reply points to the Absolute Oneness where all discriminations are transcended. It is nothing else but the experience of the great void, vast and boundless. Master Tettsu, however, did not easily approve it, and demanded, "It is not enough. Speak further!" Keizan answered again, "When I am thirsty, I drink. When I am hungry, I eat." Master Tettsu was now satisfied and verified Keizan's satori, saying, "In the future you will certainly promote Sōtō Zen."

For the ordinary mind of drinking tea and eating rice to be Tao and Zen, it has to go once and for all through the absolute negation of "A jet-black iron ball speeds through the dark night." Unless one has personally experienced the Absolute Oneness, vast and boundless, and has returned to his ordinary mind, his Tao is not true Tao which he can freely and creatively use and enjoy every day.[97]

The two statements of Keizan, "When I am thirsty I drink. When I am hungry I eat" and "A jet-black iron ball speeds through the dark night," are identical. "The Absolute Oneness where all discriminations are transcended," the "great void, vast and boundless," *is* for Keizan the "ordinary mind of drinking tea and eating rice." Hisamatsu called the one who drinks tea knowing he or she is also the "great void, vast and boundless," the "Nothingness-Subject." Fifteen years have subtracted nothing from my memory of Ryūtarō Kitahara trying to help mend my afflicted heart, hands passing over the restaurant table, proclaiming, in ecstasy: "The bowls, the cups, the glasses, the eel—*all* are emptiness." I wanted to talk about despair. He kept parrying with things' announcing their persistent splendor.

But until this is true it is a lie.

I met Hisamatsu once in my life—he was eighty-eight; I've never seen anyone so delighted at being alive. The ambivalence I felt between wanting that delight and the fear of the struggle that lay ahead if I were to attain it convulsed me in tears halfway back to Kyoto. No one volunteers to be, as he describes the moment prior to his awakening, "black, and with no means of escape left open in the entirety of his existence, not even one the size of the hole in a needle." Nor can one willingly endure one's consciousness and being as the aperture of a camera trying to close itself, as U. G. Krishnamurti described the moment antecedent to his. But the method of "cornered, then passing through," which Zen expresses with the dictum "At the root of the great doubt lies the great awakening," is, I believe, the only "path" there *can* be. The deadlocked "I," at the extremity of its unbearability, as DeMartino liked to say, no longer can bear the weight of itself and breaks up. Its breaking up is its breaking through. No one sets out on this path intentionally. To the contrary, we line up and explode out of the starting gate. After a while we check our progress and find we are in the starting gate. So we intensify our effort, monitor how far we have come, find we are in the starting gate still. This drives us to greater effort. The starting gate clings to our heels. So we make greater effort, including the effort of "letting go." But the starting gate is not something one can leave through forward motion. The trapdoor giving way—in the last failed effort to break from the starting gate—is the only way.

The introduction to the Penguin edition of W. Somerset Maugham's *The Razor's Edge* informs us that the translation of the verse from the *Katha Upanishad* that fronts his novel—

> The sharp edge of a razor is difficult to pass over;
> thus the wise say the path to Salvation is hard

—is not quite accurate. "The sense of the original . . . is that you are bound to suffer whether you stand *or* tread on the infinitesimally narrow path that can be likened to the edge of a razor."[98] Cut if you remain where you are. Cut if you move. Such is the ascent of Everest, but whether one reaches the summit as Edmund Hillary did in 1953, or freezes to death on its slopes as did George Mallory twenty-nine years prior, cannot in advance be known.

ENDNOTES

1   Walter Lowrie, *Short Life of Kierkegaard* (Princeton: University Press, 1970), p. 86.

2   Friedrich Nietzsche, "On the Genealogy of Morals," in *Basic Writings of Nietzsche*, trans. and ed. Walter Kaufmann (New York: Modern Library, 1992), p. 598. And in Friedrich Nietzsche, *The Gay Science*, trans. Walter Kaufmann (New York: Vintage, 1974), p. 125.

3   Richard DeMartino, "The Human Situation and Zen Buddhism," in D. T. Suzuki, Erich Fromm, and Richard DeMartino, *Zen Buddhism and Psychoanalysis* (New York: Harper and Brothers, 1960), pp. 156–57.

4   *The Confessions of Saint Augustine*, trans. Edward Bouverie Pusey (Whitefish, MT: Kessinger Publishing, LLC, 2004), p. 1.

5   Ibid., p. 37.

6   Shin'ichi Hisamatsu, "Hontō no Jiko ni Mezameru [Awakening to the True Self]," in *Hisamatsu Shin'ichi Chosaku-shū* [The Collected Works of Shin'ichi Hisamatsu], vol. 2 (Tokyo: Risō-sha, 1969–80), pp. 45–46.

7   Paul Tillich, *The Courage to Be* (New Haven: Yale University Press, 1952), p. 65.

8   Paul Tillich, "The Theological Significance of Existentialism and Psychoanalysis," in *Theology of Culture* (Oxford: Oxford University Press, 1959), pp. 122–23.

9   Tillich, *The Courage to Be*, p. 64.

10 Unpublished translation by Urs App. For another English translation see Franz Kafka, *Letters to Milena*, trans. Tania and James Stern (London and New York: Schocken, 1953), pp. 188–89.

11 Jiddu Krishnamurti, "The Need to Be Alone," in *Think on These Things*, ed. D. Rajagopal (New York: HarperPerennial, 1989).

12 Daisetz Teitaro Suzuki, *Essays in Zen Buddhism: Second Series* (New Delhi: Munshiram Manoharlal Publishers Pvt. Ltd, 2000), p. 107.

13 D. H. Lawrence, *Lady Chatterley's Lover* (New York: Barnes and Noble Classics, 2005), p. 186.

14 D. H. Lawrence, *Women in Love* (London: Penguin, 1995), p. 187.

15 Rainer Maria Rilke, *Duino Elegies,* trans. J. B. Leishman and Stephen Spender (New York: W. W. Norton, 1939), p. 123.

16 For the quotations from the Eighth and Third Elegies, see *The Selected Poetry of Rainer Maria Rilke*, ed. and trans. Stephen Mitchell (New York: Vintage International, 1989), pp. 193, 163. For the First and Second Elegies, see Leishman and Spender, *Duino Elegies*, pp. 21, 31–32.

17 J. P. Hodin, *Edvard Munch* (New York: Oxford University Press, 1972), pp. 86, 87.

18 Søren Kierkegaard, *Fear and Trembling* and *The Sickness Unto Death*, trans. Walter Lowrie (Princeton: Princeton University Press, 1968), p. 160.

19 *The Journal of Eugène Delacroix*, trans. Walter Pach (New York: Viking, 1972), p. 57. Actually, Michelangelo was not as close to the brink of the grave as either man thought. He lived another ten years, until 1564.

20 The italics are Twain's; the ellipses are mine. Mark Twain, *The Mysterious Stranger and Other Stories* (New York: Dover Publications, Inc., 1992), pp. 120–21.

21 Hodin, *Edvard Munch*, p. 88.

22 See Maurice Nadeau, *The Greatness of Flaubert*; Enid Starkie, Flaubert: *The Making of the Master*; Herbert Lottman, *Flaubert: A Biography*.

23 DeMartino, "The Human Situation and Zen Buddhism," pp. 146, 147–48.

24 Ibid., p. 163.

25 Shin'ichi Hisamatsu, *Zen and the Fine Arts*, trans. Gishin Tokiwa (Tokyo: Kodansha International Ltd., 1971), p. 59.

26 Blaise Pascal, *Pensées*, trans. with an introduction by A. J. Krailsheimer (New York: Penguin, 1966), number 415.

27 Ibid., number 622.

28 Ibid., number 136.

29 Ibid., number 137.

30 Ibid., number 47.

31 For all quotations from this talk see Jiddu Krishnamurti, "The Need to Be Alone," pp. 199–202.

32 Franz Kafka, "The Collected Aphorisms," in *The Great Wall of China and Other Short Stories*, trans. and ed. Malcolm Pasley (London: Penguin, 1973), p. 83.

33 Franz Kafka, "He," in ibid., p. 111.

34 Lord Byron letter, Sept. 6, 1813, written to Annabella Millbanke, later Lady Byron. *Byron's Letters and Journals*, vol. 3, ed. Leslie A. Marchand (1974).

35 All quotes in this paragraph are found in Daisetz Teitaro Suzuki, *Essays in Zen Buddhism: Second Series*, pp. 112–24. All three of the figures cited are Chinese Zen masters of the thirteenth century. Mêng-shan was one of T'ien-shan's Zen teachers.

36 Mary Lutyens, *Krishnamurti: His Life and Death* (New York: St. Martin's Press, 1990), p. 181.

37 Hermann Hesse, *Siddhartha*, trans. Stanley Appelbaum (Mineola, NY: Dover Thrift Edition, 1998), pp. 9–10. Mr. Appelbaum employs "concentration" in place of the "meditation" preferred by Hilda Rosner (Bantam, pp. 16–17) and Joachim Neugroschel (Penguin Classics, pp. 16–17).

38 David Godman, ed., *Be as You Are: The Teachings of Ramana Maharshi* (London: Arkana, 1985), pp. 62–64.

39 The words in square brackets are Richard DeMartino's, from his unpublished doctoral dissertation, "The Zen Understanding of Man," p. 174. But I have quoted here the version offered by DeMartino in class rather than the abbreviated version that appears in his dissertation. Bernard Phillips was the founder of the Temple University Department of Religion. Initially a student and teacher of philosophy, he came to feel western philosophy never reached a definitive conclusion. This led him to India and Japan, where he met Hisamatsu. He later had an avid interest in Sufism.

40 Shin'ichi Hisamatsu, "Mushinron [Atheism]," in *Hisamatsu Shin'ichi Chosaku-shū* [The Collected Works of Shin'ichi Hisamatsu], vol. 2, p. 57.

41 Shin'ichi Hisamatsu, "Shūkyō no Rêzon Dêtoru toshite no Kaku [Awakening as the Raison d'être of Religion]," in *Hisamatsu Shin'ichi Chosaku-shū* [The Collected Works of Shin'ichi Hisamatsu], vol. 2, p. 210.

42 Hisamatsu, "Atheism," p. 58.

43 Ibid.

44 Ibid., p. 59.

45 Ibid.

46 Ryūtarō Kitahara, "Makujikiko [Straight Ahead!]," in *Zen Bunka* 97 (June 1980): 35.

47 Quoted by Hisamatsu in "Mondō: At the Death of a 'Great-Death-Man,'" in *A Zen Life: D. T. Suzuki Remembered*, photographs by Francis Haar, ed. Masao Abe (New York: Weatherhill, 1986), p. 146.

48 See Part One, p. 7.

49 "Dialogues, East and West: Paul Tillich and Shin'ichi Hisamatsu," trans. and ed. Richard DeMartino, p. 50. Reference is to the unpublished revised version. Originally published in three parts in *The Eastern Buddhist*, new series, no. 4 (October 1971): 89–107; no. 5 (October 1972): 107–28; no. 6 (October 1973): 87–114.

50 Shin'ichi Hisamatsu, "The Vow of Humankind (3)," *F.A.S. Society Journal* (Kyoto) (Autumn 1987): 6. Trans. Christopher Ives.

51 Shin'ichi Hisamatsu, "Jinrui no Chikai [The Vow of Humankind]," in *Hisamatsu Shin'ichi Chosaku-shū* [The Collected Works of Shin'ichi Hisamatsu], vol. 3, pp. 248–49.

52 *The Complete Works of Chuang Tzu*, trans. Burton Watson (New York: Columbia University Press, 1968), pp. 234–35.

53 U. G. Krishnamurti, *The Mystique of Enlightenment*, ed. Rodney Arms (Boulder: Sentient Publications, LLC, 2002), pp. 120, 122. It seems desirable in writing this footnote to include what Mr. Krishnamurti writes on the inside page: "My teaching, if that is the word you want to use, has no copyright. You are free to reproduce, distribute, interpret, misinterpret, distort, garble, do what you like, even claim authorship, without my consent or the permission of anybody."

54 Shin'ichi Hisamatsu, "Mumonkan Dai-issoku Teikō [A Talk on the First Case of the Mumonkan]," in *Hisamatsu Shin'ichi Chosaku-shū*, vol. 3, p. 637. The thoroughgoing sundering of all routes is of such significance to Hisamatsu that at the end of his commentary on the first case of the Wumenkuan (Mumonkan) he returns to this theme—and only this theme— saying: "This 'bringing the routes of the mind [and body] to the extremity, and then extinguishing them'—in other words, having oneself driven into a total deadlock without the slightest possibility of advance—is not in any sense easily attained. Nonetheless, it is not impossible to accomplish" (Hisamatsu, ibid., p. 644). It must be noted that this "accomplishment" is not an achievement of the will of the ordinary "I." It is attained, rather, through the final expenditure of the "I" and its will by exacerbating to its limit the contradiction between the attempt to cut off all routes and the inability to do so.

55 DeMartino, "The Human Situation and Zen Buddhism," p. 167.

56 Lutyens, *Krishnamurti: His Life and Death*, p. 157.

57 Ibid., pp. 185–86.

58 Richard DeMartino in a classroom lecture, 1984.

59 *The Unabridged Journals of Sylvia Plath*, ed. Karen V. Kukil (New York: Anchor Books, 2000), p. 31.

60 Paul Tillich in *The Courage to Be* analyzes three forms of negation (or "nonbeing") which threaten to nullify our attempts at self-affirmation: death, emptiness-meaninglessness, and the guilt or self-condemnation of failing to become what one knows one must be. Loneliness, it seems to me, is an equal fourth. As works like Wagner's *The Flying Dutchman*, Swift's *Gulliver's Travels*, and Werner Herzog's film *Nosferatu* show, the inability to die, so long as the lonely interiority of self-consciousness is not transcended, can be hell. Perhaps the concept of negation can be better understood by contemplating Malraux's remark in *Man's Fate*: "The great mystery is not that we should have been thrown here at random between the profusion of matter and that of the stars; it is that from our very prison we can draw, from our own selves, images powerful enough to deny our nothingness." The fact that there is no guarantee that in a given life nothingness (negation) will be "denied"—in other words, surmounted—should make the meaning of the phrase negating force clear.

61 Paul Tillich, *Love, Power, and Justice* (London: Oxford University Press, 1954), p. 40.

62 U. G. Krishnamurti, *The Mystique of Enlightenment*, p. 124.

63 Quoted in Lawrence Durrell, *Justine* (New York: Pocket Books, 1961), p. 227. Durrell indicates his translation is "by no means literal."

64 Ego, again, not in the Freudian sense, but ego as the Latin word for "I."

65 DeMartino, "The Human Situation and Zen Buddhism" (revised version), in *Buddhist and Western Psychology*, ed. Nathan Katz (Boulder: Prajna Press, 1983), p. 185.

66 U. G. Krishnamurti, *The Mystique of Enlightenment*, p. 27.

67 "Shōzan-Rōshi and Contemporary Zen," *F.A.S. Zen Society Newsletter* (Kyoto) (Spring 1978): 1–2. Trans. Howard Curtis. Translation slightly modified. See "Shōzan-Rōshi to Gendai no Zen [Shōzan-Rōshi and Contemporary Zen]," *Zen Bunka* 86 (September 1977): 28–29, for the Japanese text of this interview with Hisamatsu.

68 Ibid.

69 Shin'ichi Hisamatsu, "Hontō no Jiko ni Mezameru [Awakening to the True Self]," in *Hisamatsu Shin'ichi Chosaku-shū* [The Collected Works of Shin'ichi Hisamatsu], vol. 2, pp. 45–46.

70 Ibid., p. 45.

71 Shin'ichi Hisamatsu, "Kakutai [Awakened Subjectivity]," in *Hisamatsu Shin'ichi Chosaku-shū* [The Collected Works of Shin'ichi Hisamatsu], vol. 2, p. 321. See also Pai-chang Huai-hai: "[U]nborn, imperishable . . . this is called birth, old age, sickness and death." *Sayings and Doings of Pai-chang: Chan Master of Great Wisdom*, trans. Thomas Cleary (Los Angeles: Center Publications, 1979), p. 75.

72 Shin'ichi Hisamatsu, "Ultimate Crisis and Resurrection: Part One," *The Eastern Buddhist*, n.s., 8 (May 1975), p. 29. Trans. Gishin Tokiwa.

73 Hisamatsu, "Atheism," p. 85.

74 "Dialogues: Hisamatsu and Tillich," p. 58.

75 Quoted in Shin'ichi Hisamatsu, "Zen: Its Meaning for Modern Civilization," in *The Eastern Buddhist*, n.s., 1 (September 1965), p. 44. Trans. Richard DeMartino and Gishin Tokiwa. The quotation comes from the Pure Land Sutra.

76 Hisamatsu, "Awakening as the Raison d'Être of Religion," p. 219.

77 See M. Conrad Hyers, *Zen and the Comic Spirit* (Westminster: John Knox Press, 1975). I no longer have the book in my possession and do not know the page number.

78 "The calm should be found within the turbulence and not in escaping from it. In other words, it ought to be one's Calm Self that is working in the activity." "Of far greater importance [than transitory meditation-induced composure], and this goes to the heart of Zen, is to be able under the strain of strenuous effort to enjoy an undisturbed tranquility." "When awakened to the Calm Self, the hustle and bustle or commotion around you is nothing to you" ("Dialogues: Tillich and Hisamatsu," pp. 5–6).

79 Shin'ichi Hisamatsu, "The Vow of Humankind (2)," *F.A.S. Society Journal* (Kyoto) (Winter 1986–87): 29. Trans. Christopher Ives. Translation slightly modified. See also Hisamatsu, "Jinrui no Chikai [The Vow of Humankind]," vol. 3, pp. 231–32.

80 Shin'ichi Hisamatsu, "Za to iu koto o chūshin ni [A Discussion Centering Around Zen Meditation]," in *Hisamatsu Shin'ichi Chosaku-shū* [The Collected Works of Shin'ichi Hisamatsu], vol. 3, p. 653.

81 "Dialogues: Tillich and Hisamatsu," p. 42.

82 Hisamatsu, "Ultimate Crisis and Resurrection: Part Two," in *The Eastern Buddhist*, n.s., 8 (October 1975), p. 51. Trans. Gishin Tokiwa.

83 Shin'ichi Hisamatsu, "Zen to wa nani ka [What Is Zen?]," in *Hisamatsu Shin'ichi Chosaku-shū* [The Collected Works of Shin'ichi Hisamatsu], vol. 8, p. 420.

84 Shin'ichi Hisamatsu, "Kōteki Mujōkan [Affirmative View of Transience]," in *Hisamatsu Shin'ichi Chosaku-shū* [The Collected Works of Shin'ichi Hisamatsu], vol. 2, p. 259.

85 Hisamatsu reading from his autobiographical account in "Shōzan-Rōshi and Contemporary Zen."

86 Shin'ichi Hisamatsu, "The Characteristics of Oriental Nothingness," trans. Richard DeMartino in collaboration with Jikai Fujiyoshi and Masao Abe in *Philosophical Studies of Japan* 2 (1960), p. 76.

87 Hisamatsu, *Zen and the Fine Arts*, p. 48.

88 Hesse, *Siddhartha*, trans. Appelbaum, p. 77.

89 Quoted in Martin Lings, *A Sufi Saint of the Twentieth Century* (Berkeley: University of California Press, 1973), pp. 127, 160.

90 Stephen Jourdain, *Radical Awakening*, ed. Gilles Farcet (Carlsbad, CA: Inner Directions Publications, 2001), pp. 192, 135, 118, 120, 123.

91 *The Complete Works of Chuang Tzu*, trans. Burton Watson, p. 83.

92 *The Rubaiyat of Omar Khayyam*, trans. Edward Fitzgerald (stanza li).

93 Unpublished account of Dr. Urs App's meeting with Hisamatsu in 1979. Dr. App was the last westerner to meet Hisamatsu before his death.

94 Quoted in D. T. Suzuki, "Lectures in Zen Buddhism," in D. T. Suzuki, Erich Fromm, and Richard DeMartino, *Zen Buddhism and Psychoanalysis* (New York: Harper and Brothers, 1960), p. 16.

95 Speaking of the T'ang dynasty master, Lin-chi, Hisamatsu says: "Even if he wasn't approached in any way or didn't move a finger, his answer is already out before he was questioned." Shin'ichi Hisamatsu, "On the Record of Rinzai (2)," in *The Eastern Buddhist*, n.s. 14 (Autumn 1981). Trans. Gishin Tokiwa and Christopher A. Ives. p. 15. Translation slightly modified. See also Hisamatsu, "Rinzai Roku Shōkō," in *Hisamatsu Shin'ichi Chosaku-shū* [The Collected Works of Shin'ichi Hisamatsu], vol. 6, p. 210.

96 Hisamatsu, "Mondō: At the Death of a 'Great-Death Man,'" p. 147. Translation slightly modified. See Shin'ichi Hisamatsu, "Daishitei no Hito [Great Death Man]," in *Hisamatsu Shin'ichi Chosaku-shū* [The Collected Works of Shin'ichi Hisamatsu], vol. 2, p. 128, for the Japanese text.

97 Zenkei Shibayama, *Zen Comments on the Mumonkan*, trans. Sumiko Kudo (New York: Harper and Row, 1974), p. 150.

98 W. Somerset Maugham, *The Razor's Edge*, introduction by Anthony Curtis (Middlesex: Penguin Books, 1992), p. xvii.

ABOUT THE AUTHOR

STEVE ANTINOFF HAS a doctorate in religion. He lived in Japan for many years, where he studied Zen Buddhism. He currently teaches philosophy and religion at the University of the Arts in Philadelphia.